D0943179

Buhler, Walther, author.
 Living with your body

FEB 13 2015

DATE DUE

GAYLORD   #3523PI   Printed in USA

LIVING WITH YOUR BODY

Health, Illness and Understanding the Human Being

WALTHER BÜHLER

RUDOLF STEINER PRESS

Rudolf Steiner Press
Hillside House, The Square
Forest Row, RH18 5ES

www.rudolfsteinerpress.com

Published by Rudolf Steiner Press 2013

First published in English in 1979. Second edition 1982. Reprinted 2013

Originally publised in German by Verlag Freies Geistesleben, Stuttgart, in 1978

© Walther Bühler 1978
This translation © Rudolf Steiner Press 1982

Translated from German by L. Maloney

The moral right of the author has been asserted under the Copyright, Designs and Patents Act, 1988

A catalogue record for this book is available from the British Library

ISBN 978 1 85584 390 5

Cover by Andrew Morgan Design
Printed and bound in Great Britain by 4edge Ltd, Essex

CONTENTS

FOREWORD

Despite the progress mankind has made in all areas of life, civilization is tending towards an increasing superficiality, while the threat to physical existence on the earth grows. Yet man himself is still in many ways an unknown being. This book will help to awaken a new interest in a deeper understanding for this human being.

No one can escape the urgent questions of this time. How to lead one's life and conduct one's work in a meaningful way; nutrition and all it involves; the individual's relationship to his fellow men; the question of destiny, of sickness and health—these are inescapable issues concerning the hygiene of life in its widest sense. What are the yardsticks and views we can use today to guide us through the chaos of out-dated and conflicting concepts and the general hurly-burly of life?

Instincts have become unreliable and even people in positions of leadership have allowed their consciousness to be restricted by materialistic concepts. It is no longer possible to place the responsibility for life's decisions on other's shoulders, leaving everything to the 'experts' or some government body or institution. We have all become seekers!

Descriptions, such as those in this book, which give a direction for the quest, are therefore of the utmost value. The sick will be particularly helped by this new picture of the human being that will assist them to understand their illness and see the sense of therapies based on natural as well as spiritual considerations. Efforts to lead a more healthy life, which to people outside the medical profession often seem rather pointless, become meaningful. Teachers, therapists, nurses and parents will appreciate the deeper understanding that provides a more solid basis for their work.

H. H. VOGEL, M.D.

Chapter One

THE THREEFOLD NATURE OF THE HUMAN ORGANISM

Man's superiority to other natural beings is to be looked for less in the perfection of his outer form than in his inner life: that is, his life of soul and spirit, his power of consciousness, his reason. It is because of these inner endowments that he develops in his own unique way, achieving mastery over the rest of nature, and striving also to master his own destiny. Yet all his faculties of soul and spirit, crowned in self-awareness, are bound up with his organism; and his fate is therefore in large measure dependent upon the correct functioning of his body: that is, upon conditions of bodily *health* and *sickness*.

Ever again man asks the age-old question: 'How does the soul actually live in the body? Where, in which organ, is the seat of the soul?' We shall try to formulate some fundamental thoughts on these questions from the physician's point of view. For how we take care of our health and live our lives, how we fit into the circle of our family and friends or find our place in humanity as a whole, is in many respects dependent upon the image we have of ourselves.

Views on the relationship of soul and body have changed greatly in the course of time. In recent decades those medical and biological scientists who still retain some vestige of feeling for man's spiritual nature have increasingly adopted the view that the brain is the seat of the soul. This view is supported by the fact that malfunctioning or, under certain conditions, sudden loss of consciousness is the direct result of the failure or malfunctioning of some process in the brain. If someone's brain is receiving an inadequate supply of blood, because of low blood pressure for example, and if the air in the room becomes a bit stale, he may faint—just because his brain is receiving insufficient blood. All his other organs may be functioning properly, yet the whole man enters a sleep-like state from which he cannot be aroused by ordinary means. In any case, his thoughts, feelings, and will—and thus his whole inner life—are temporarily extinguished.

Such phenomena—supported by observations, of old people for example, whose calcified, narrowed arteries no longer adequately supply the brain with oxygenated blood—make clear the soul's dependence upon the functioning of the brain. In such cases, intellectual and spiritual life is no longer what it once was; memory and power of retention no longer function correctly. The person may lose his natural self-awareness, and with it the ability to shape his life through thought. Because his other organs are relatively healthy, he may live another ten years; but because his brain is calcified, his soul can no longer properly express itself. Many similar observations, along with much more complicated, more precise examinations of the brain and of the nerves issuing from it, have led some scientists to conclude that all soul life is connected with the brain.

In a time when materialism was even deeper than it is today, it was said that the brain processes themselves produce the life of the soul and consciousness. Many still believe that the brain, like the blossoming flower that gives off a fragrance at the highest stage in its development, exudes, so to speak, the fragrance of the soul. With as much or as little significance as the fragrance of the flower, which naturally disappears when the flower fades, the soul is felt to be mortal and totally ephemeral because it is bound up with the body. Thus we see that posing the question as to the seat of the soul leads us to fundamental questions of importance to everyone, questions everyone has asked himself in a quiet moment: 'Why am I here; what is the meaning of my life; does life continue after death, or has it been lived in vain because death brings it to an end?' Because such questions deeply affect a man's general frame of mind and attitude towards life, especially if they are answered in the negative, they also influence community life and social organization.

Let us now approach the problem of body and soul from a completely different point of view. Just as we know from the outdoors that there are clouds, flowers, and stones, so we know from inner experience that our own inner life, which is also observable to some extent, takes on various forms and has various potentialities. When we behold an image from the past within ourselves, we know it is connected with our memory, with our recollection. Such images are flexible; we can alter them, transform them, relate them to one another—and then we say that we are *thinking*. However, if some inner image fills us with a feeling of joy, of pleasure, of sympathy, antipathy or fear, then we know our soul can also *feel*. And if this feeling becomes still stronger—if, perhaps, antipathy develops into hatred, or liking into an ardent desire to possess something—then we note how eager we are, how we perhaps feel compelled by something, how we translate thought into *deed*. We then experience ourselves inwardly as human beings who will and act. In other words, the life of the soul manifests itself in thinking, that is, in producing images and forming ideas; in feeling, which oscillates between desire and aversion, joy and sorrow; and in willing.

Now we must ask: 'What is the relationship of this life of the soul to a man's outward appearance, to what each of us possesses as his physical body?' Let us first consider willing, the act of will, by observing ourselves or someone else at work. When we go into a garden and watch the gardener digging up a beet, pulling out dead flowers, moving soil, sowing seeds, and pushing a wheelbarrow around, we confront the activity of a man's will. He moves the materials of his environment; he brings them towards himself or pushes them away; he reshapes them. But a man can do this only by moving himself, by having a certain mobility of his own. He is not a marble statue that stands there, rigid, moving its surroundings by magic; no, he needs the mobility of his own body, of his torso, in order to reach out into the material world through movement. If a man is unaccustomed to such work—for the activity of a man's will, if it is meaningful, is work—if he comes home from the office and then helps out in a garden or in a quarry, two days later he may suddenly find himself in severe pain. We know this pain as muscular stiffness. It is a good thing that man can experience such stiffness, for he notices in this simple way that muscles are necessary for the activity of his will. Where would we be without our muscular system!

Yet these muscles would be powerless to contract, become hard, and then to relax and become soft again if they could not make full use of the resistance supplied by rigid bone. Because the muscles are attached to bones by tendons, they have the firm support necessary to release their energy outwards. We observe that the bones, in turn, are rendered mobile through the joints, the ligaments, and so forth. So we discover what might be called the *limb system*, comprising all the tubular bones, as these are connected by joints, and moved with the help of muscles. The way the will works and lives, the use it makes of muscles as the instrument of its activity—in short, the whole limb system—is easily understood. We have all felt its reality through the common experience of muscular stiffness. Thus, in so far as our soul manifests will-forces, it lives in the limbs.

It is remarkable, then, that man has muscles that function despite the fact that they are not governed by his free will. We can pick up some food, divide it into small pieces, and bring it to our mouths. We can continue this voluntary activity by chewing, pushing the food around with the tongue and working it into a uniform mass, then swallowing it. Voluntary muscle activity goes this far. But the moment the mouthful of food is swallowed, a different kind of activity begins. The food slides down the oesophagus and is further processed in the stomach; it then passes into the intestine and ultimately, after travelling a complicated route and undergoing many transformations, into the blood and the liver.

When we study this processing, transporting, and conversion of food substance, we notice that none of this activity would be possible without muscles. The oesophagus is, after all, a muscular tube; the stomach is in some respects a sack, but its walls are structured in a marvellous way, having not only a mucous membrane, but also fine layers of muscles arranged in a specific configuration and capable of exerting considerable force. And when food in liquid form is pushed along, concentrated, and then dispersed again in rhythmic movements over the large surface areas of the intestine, all this is once again muscular activity. Thus we find in these muscles an active force that must be called a kind of will—but one that is not affected by the conscious life of the soul. We can speak here of *unconscious* will-forces and begin to understand how, through them, our life of soul takes root deep within the body. These willforces go on working in the gross movements and transformations of food that take place during digestion itself, as well as in the increasingly delicate metabolic activity of the liver, blood, and circulation. Yet we must understand that these movements are not merely mechanical; they are directed by the power of man's will.

To summarize, in addition to the activity of the will in the limbs, there is an inner, unconscious, organically-rooted will activity that takes place in the metabolic processes, in the 'metabolic system'. So when we look at the whole man, we can say that both his limbs and his metabolic system are the physical basis and instruments of his will.

The main organs of the metabolic system—the stomach, the intestines, the liver, and so forth—are below the diaphragm. Everything is in motion in the organs of this body cavity. The stomach moves as soon as it begins functioning. The small intestine is also in motion; and the intestinal loops have no fixed orientation, but can move about vigorously. Even such organs as the spleen and liver can expand and contract again—we notice the part played by the spleen in digestion or in movements of the limbs when we get a stitch in the side while running. At such times, we become partly aware of the will activity in this organ, activity that otherwise remains unconscious. The gall bladder functions similarly, expanding and contracting in 'manipulations' of which we remain unconscious. Through these movements it discharges the sharp and bitter gall that breaks down foodstuffs.

My main concern has been to show that all that

takes place in the area of the abdomen and limbs is accompanied by mobility and movement. The organs of this region work together and can be collectively designated as the *metabolic-limb system*. It is this system that builds up man's body, continually supplying it with new substances that enter the body through the roundabout course traced by the anabolic forces of the blood. We know indeed, that much of the blood is prepared in the limbs themselves, through important processes in the innermost part of the limbs, the bone marrow. Red blood cells and certain white blood corpuscles are produced there, just as blood proteins, blood sugar, and other substances are prepared in the liver and other organs. And the blood itself is a living tissue continuously in motion. Deep-seated forces of the *will* are active in all such mobility of organs.

*

There is another, totally different aspect of man, opposite the one we have just presented. The anatomist speaks of three body cavities in man, one of which we have briefly considered. The other two are the thoracic, or chest, cavity and the cranial, or head, cavity. Let us now examine the latter. The brain, a very complex organ, lies within the cranial cavity. Although it is relatively small, medical students find that they need to put more time and effort into studying it than into learning about all the organs of the abdominal cavity put together.

What is the nature of the brain? It is an unusually

pale, grey organ; if you ever have the opportunity of seeing the brain and how it is situated in the skull, you will be inadvertently reminded of the coiled appearance of the intestine. For here we see nothing but coils, extraordinary structures that merge with one another—even as we speak of the coils or convolutions of the brain. But despite its appearance, even the outward form of the brain is quite different from that of the intestine. For, to our great surprise, this organ does not move at all. All these convolutions are fixed with respect to one another. The millions of brain cells with their many fibres, ramifications, and extensions—which we observe and call nerves and which, issuing from the brain, extend throughout the body—are absolutely immobile. They are as immobile as, for example, the wires strung between telephone poles. And unlike the liver or the spleen, the whole brain as an organ must not expand or contract by so much as a millimetre. If it does, we immediately get an excruciating headache —in other words, we are no longer healthy. When we lift our gaze to the human head, we observe that here the mobility that was characteristic of the metabolic-limb system has come almost to a standstill.

We can see this lack of mobility also in the twenty skull bones: they all firmly interlock—with one exception—so that there can be no flexibility or movement. They are held in place in a very complex fashion by sutures that allow no chance of displacement, so that a rigid structure, immobile within itself, is created. The cranial cavity is something like a jail, in which the brain sits so closely confined that it even leaves a partial imprint of its convolutions in the bone. It cannot move at all, because the bone itself confines it and holds it in place.

The bones of the skull are completely different also in shape from those of the limbs. The limb bones are arranged radially and are columnar in form, even in the spinal column, while the bones of the skull are bowl-shaped and form a structure that does not reach out from the body but curves and closes to form a kind of hollow ball. A roughly spherical structure is created. Thus the skull dissociates itself from the mobility and activity of the rest of the body and enters a state of rigidity and repose. Thereby the head presents a great contrast to the limbs. This contrast is manifested in many ways, some of which I shall touch upon now.

When the stomach or the hand are active, they need matter upon which to act. The task of the metabolic-limb system is to reach out into the material world, the world of weight and mass, and to set this world in motion, bring it closer, and transform it. The stomach wants to be filled with matter in one form or another: it requires something to knead and process. Contrast this with the way the head reacts to matter. We can observe this reaction very readily at dinner. With the help of the hand, the head is supplied with food, thereby taking a small loan from the limb system. It brings into play its own limited joint system: the only movable bone of the head, forming the lower jaw. But once it has taken in a mouthful of some substance and chewed it, the head has nothing more pressing to do than expel this substance from its own sphere of activity, the oral cavity, by swallowing it. It then says to the stomach, 'Now you take a crack at it! I don't want to have anything more to do with it.' Then the head turns to taking in finer substances that are easier to process: it breathes in air. Yet scarcely has it noticed what the air is like—whether it is fragrant, fresh, or stifling— when it no longer wants the air and sends it off too, though not so far as the foodstuffs, namely down into the chest cavity via the trachea. The head wants to have nothing more to do with the air. If air approaches the head by a different route, through the ear, for example, the head appears to let it in. But it actually sets up another barrier. How much of the air that enters the auditory canal does the head really let in? Everything material—the substance of the air beating against it—it closes out through the boundary set by the ear drum. The head allows only the very finest parts of the air to enter: rhythm, vibration, tone. These alone the head lets in.

So we see that there is a relationship between the head and the world, but one in which the head rejects everything that could weigh it down by, or bind it up with, matter and substance, accepting only what is not substantial: from food, only the sensation of taste—sweet, sour, or bitter; from the air, only tone or fragrance. Finally, the head opens up to the whole world through the eye. But what does it take in? Only impressions of light and colour—the *forms* that the individual elements of the material world take on, but not the substances themselves.

What, then, does the head actually retain from its numerous encounters with the world? It retains only images. And these images are no longer reality; they are, so to speak, photographs or silhouettes of the surrounding world. We preserve these images very carefully with the aid of our memory, so that our soul can call them up time and again, to revivify them. It is clear that our head relates to the world in a manner completely different from the limbs. In a certain sense, the head leads a special quite aristocratic, life. What, then, is its task? Where have all the forces gone through which the organism acts on the material world in the liver, stomach, and limbs?

Before returning to this question we must look once again at the metabolic system. Consider, for example, the chemical effect the stomach has on the material world through its production of such juices as hydrochloric acid. What great forces are at work here! We have mentioned that these are not only digestive, but also anabolic forces, connected with the formation of blood. We find anabolism at work where a wound is being healed or where cells are being created or regenerated. And what happens when the organism brings all these anabolic forces together and concentrates them on a single task? The alliance of all anabolic forces creates the highest development of which the forces of blood, will, and metabolism are capable. This is no relatively minor occurrence, such as the transformation of a small amount of some substance or the generation of a small piece of new skin, but the creation of a *whole new human being*. In this act all the life-building forces are gathered together so that an entirely new organism can come into being via the reproductive organs, an organism that is formed and moulded from matter. I should like to add reproduction to our observations of the metabolic system. We may even say that the highest development of this *lower* man—so called in contrast to the *upper* man—is its ability to propagate the species.

Without mitosis (cell division) and without the careful nurturing of the cell itself, the building block of life for any organism, reproduction would be unthinkable. We can replace a small piece of skin or create a whole man only because the cells are capable of division and reproduction.

Returning now to the head, we see in a new way that its situation is polaric to that of the metabolic-reproductive systems. The situation in the head is just the opposite. What happens there? Not even *one* brain cell can divide; no hole in the brain or loss of substance can be compensated. In this respect, too, the brain is unique. Within a few weeks of birth, the brain cells have become incapable of mitosis, inner regeneration, or reproduction. We could say that the magnificent activity shown by the lower organism of man, in the formation of blood, the multiplication of cells, and reproduction itself, gradually diminishes until it ceases entirely in the head. Here is the realm of the nerves, the organic opposite of the blood. Not only external mobility ceases here, not only the ability to move substances, but even the capacity to regenerate and reproduce.

There are many other examples of this opposition between the head and the metabolic-limb system. The results of such observations are always the same: if we picture the opposite of everything that takes place in the lower man, we know what will be happening in the head. Why is it that the forces of life are so weak in the head, that the head attaches so little importance to nutrition, reproduction, regeneration, or movement, that everything seems there to be in a state of paralysis and rigidity? One is almost tempted to say that a kind of laziness in the organism is manifest in the brain. Or should we say that the brain is not really healthy? For when a being is not active and can no longer reproduce or heal itself, one is really tempted to say it is no longer healthy.

But surely the head cannot have such a negative function. What, then, is its positive task?

If we study the head carefully, we see that it is actually quite mobile, and productive, too. I am not referring to the fact that the head turns on the neck: that is done by the limbs and their muscles. The head's mobility lies in a totally different sphere. We find it when we notice that we can form thoughts in the head and move them around. We can inwardly recall an image and dismiss it again; we can recall another image, or even two, and associate them with one another. Through the faculties of the head we can travel on to far-off lands or return to the distant past. In other words, the inner life of the head is incredibly mobile. The things it moves have been freed of substance and exist on a completely non-material plane. Living in the wealth of its images, the head is active, formative, even creative; we might well say that it is *at work*. If we call work a shaping, transforming, moving, ordering and handling with care, then the head works, because it acts in all these ways upon its images. The head does with images what the lower man does with the substances of the outer world. We are referring to remembering, using the imagination, developing thoughts—in general, to thinking.

We could sum up these capabilities, so familiar to all of us, with the expression 'forming ideas'. In this process, the soul frees itself as much as possible from the processes of metabolism and devotes its energy to processing the mental images that form the content of its own experience. In the head, the body does not hold back the soul-forces; instead, it frees them for independent work (see Figure 1). For this reason alone the soul's conscious life can shine forth in all its inner richness; from the head the soul can govern the rest of the body. Thus the head, though incapable of organic regeneration and reproduction, brings man forth a second time, but on a higher plane: as a self-aware spiritual being, as a personality.

We are correct in saying that the soul's instrument for thinking and forming ideas is the head, or more accurately, the brain and the nervous system. These in turn would be unthinkable without the sense organs, the portals through which they in their own way take hold of the world. All the most important sense organs are located in the head and are connected there through the nerves to that marvellous structure, the brain. The *sensory-nervous system,* then, in so far as it is concentrated in the *upper* man, constitutes the other great pole of man's being. As the seat of his activity of ideation this system of nerves and senses is the diametric opposite of the metabolic-limb system (see Figure 1).

*

Man's life of soul has yet a third possibility, which we have touched upon only briefly: that of feeling. We will come to understand feeling if we experience it inwardly as lying midway between thinking and willing. Just consider for a moment what must happen for a thought, a mere image, to become a reality in the outer, material world. Let us say you have a thought, perhaps a very beautiful, clear one: for example, a right-angled object, the image of which appears in the head, and is called by it a cube or a regular solid. As yet, this object is not real in the physical sense. If it is to become a reality, the limbs must obtain the necessary material, be it wood, clay or marble. They fashion this material, and suddenly the cube is there as an external reality in the material world. The metabolic-limb system has shaped it; man's will has been activated.

How does this transformation come about? How

does a mere image become an external reality? Through the will, of course. But there must be some-

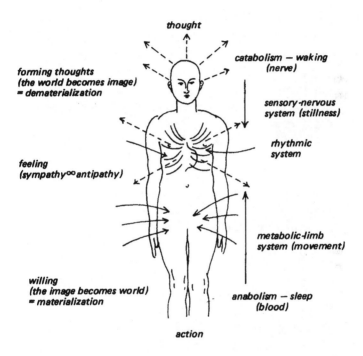

Fig. 1. The Threefold Human Organism

thing to bridge the gulf between the head and the limbs. What happens is that you inwardly develop a great liking for this cube and perhaps think to yourself, 'It's really a shame that this image is so quickly lost and that I do not have it in front of me to show to others. Couldn't I transform my thought into a reality?' From your liking for this beautiful, clear thought comes the wish: 'If only it could have a lasting existence!' You have been caught up in your feelings. And because you can feel, because you can enjoy what you have thought of or seen, you have an inner compulsion to translate it into deed, into an act of will. In this way feeling mediates between thinking and willing.

We must now ask which organs and which functions of the organism provide the physical basis for the soul's feeling. The spiritual-scientific study of man gives a totally new answer, one that may be more difficult to understand than anything we have presented thus far: Man's feeling has as its physical basis everything that originates in breathing and follows a rhythmic pattern. Let us pursue this line of thought.

You can experience and observe the truth of this assertion first hand. Let us say, for example, that you are delighted with something; you may express this feeling by starting to laugh. There is no way to do this without setting the respiratory system in motion. And if you are really delighted, you may even feel your heart 'leap for joy'. If you have a strong negative feeling, such as fear, you feel yourself turning pale. You can also read this feeling in another man's face when he turns pale. If he has a different feeling, such as anger or shame, his face turns red. Whenever a strong feeling is experienced by the soul, something takes place in the circulation, in the subtle interplay between blood and breath. If we study carefully the powerful effects of sympathy and antipathy, we shall always find that they cause subtle changes in the rhythm of circulation, heartbeat, and respiration. These changes can certainly be studied more carefully than we have done; the detailed examination of how the activities taking place in the blood and breath are connected with man's feelings remains a great task for the future. We shall take a closer look at this connection in Chapter Two.

What we have discussed with respect to the life of feeling can, however, be summed up in one organ system. Just as we have spoken of a sensory-nervous system and a metabolic-limb system, so too we may speak of a *rhythmic* system. We find rhythmic forms even in the anatomy itself, in the external form of the human body. Consider the rib cage: the wonderful, rhythmic alternation of bone and intercostal muscle. The rib cage is an intermediate structure between the head and the limbs, showing properties of both. At its lower end, near the metabolic-limb system, its form is expanded; here the ribs stretch, straighten, and seek to become limbs. Those that have become really mobile and separated themselves from the breastbone, however, are false, or floating, ribs. At the upper end of the rib cage, nearer the head, the ribs are like the bowl-shaped bones of the skull, becoming increasingly shallow and rounded, each seeking to interlock with the rib opposite. Here, at its upper end, the rib cage comes, as it were, to a head. The ribs as a whole, do not seem to know what they really want: At its lower end the rib cage wants to behave like the limbs, with full mobility and freedom. But at its upper end it is shaped, rounded, and immobile and seeks to remain at rest like the head.

The interaction of the chest with its surroundings is just as indecisive—or should I say, just as versatile. First it accepts the material world, through inhalation, and then, through exhalation, rejects it. But in order to exist, in order to remain organically healthy, the chest must strike a balance between the two poles: between absolutely rigid immobility and total mobility, as also between the taking in and giving off of substance.

What, then, creates harmony and mediates between these two extremes? A stilling of movement, a moving of stillness! It is rhythmic movement, the ordered alternation between expansion and contraction, that mediates between the two. We experience pure rhythm in the 'in' and 'out' of inhalation and exhalation, in the expansion and contraction of the heart, in the flow of arterial blood away from the heart to the extremities and the flow of venous blood back to the heart from the extremities. These rhythms of holding and letting go are the organic, physical counterparts of what takes place in the soul when we rejoice or weep, when we are happy or sad, excited or depressed. Just give it a try—for every emotion, you can think of or feel an opposite emotion. Love is the opposite of hate, liking the opposite of dislike, compassion the opposite of cruelty. Man's whole emotional life oscillates back and forth and is itself a kind of breathing or pulsating of the soul. For this reason, feeling requires an organic system that is capable of expansion and contraction, or of movement back and forth.

It should be growing clear now why the particular organs that define the rhythmic element and allow it to function are able to provide physical basis for the soul's activity and experience of itself in feeling. And just as feeling is the soul's bridge between inner image and outer reality, between inner movement in thought and external movement in will, so the body's rhythmic system, including everything in the organism that follows a rhythmic pattern, is the intermediary between 'above' and 'below'—in short, between blood and nerve.

*

We now have a complete picture of the human organism. Before us is a radiant new picture of man: Man's own being is bound up in the greatest organic polarity imaginable. But the opposite poles, which can be found even within the individual organs, must not be allowed to connect in short-circuit fashion, for the results would be catastrophic. The scales, so to speak, would tip back and forth in an unheard of way, and man would become ill in body or soul. It is *rhythm* that comes between these poles: mediating, harmonizing, and making the transition from the one to the other. Thus, the nourishment that is transformed into blood receives a rhythmic influence from the heart and breath and only thereafter is it ready to pass over into the nervous system.

Through our own empirical observations we have worked out the idea of the *threefold* nature of man's organism. We see that this organism, which outwardly appears to be unified, is inwardly dual and lives in polarity. Only when this polarity is mediated by a third force, only when man bridges the inner gulf in order to reconcile this polarity—one could almost say healing himself where he has been torn apart into opposing elements—does he become healthy. Just this rhythmic mediation between conflicting opposites is what gives rise to a physical organism fit to serve as the instrument of man's soul.

The threefoldness of man's body and its functioning reflects a corresponding division in his life of soul. If now we ask again where the soul is located, we see that we cannot single out any one organ as the seat of the soul. No, indeed! The human body from head to foot is the soul's instrument. This is one of the great discoveries made by Rudolf Steiner in his research on human life.* Anatomists and physiologists who make use of this idea need no longer content themselves with purely physical descriptions of the organs, nor need they study the body's chemical and digestive processes in isolation. Those who persist in

* The idea of the threefold human organism was presented for the first time by Rudolf Steiner in 1917, after thirty years of research, in his book *Von Seelenrätseln* (Riddles of the Soul), Rudolf Steiner Nachlassverwaltung, Dornach, 1960. See also *The Study of Man* (fourteen lectures given in 1919), Rudolf Steiner Press, London, 1966.

doing so can never overcome the materialism touched upon earlier. We must be able to say of the human organism that all its forms and processes point to something behind them, something active, creative, and self-experiencing. They point to man's soul. Living in a material body, the soul brings this matter into such magnificent articulations, combinations, and rhythms, that every aspect of the body can serve as the soul's vehicle, though of course in many different ways. And it is exactly this diversity of function that must be carefully studied if we are ever to understand the relationship between body and soul—that is, the essential in man.

In closing, let me sum up my observations in a single picture that should illustrate my whole train of thought. When the soul wills, when it wants to translate something into deed, into reality, it is like a swimmer who dives into the water, submerges, and temporarily disappears. In such a way the soul immerses itself in the material world of the organs and moves them from within. Then it is willing. But if the soul wants to discover itself, to find itself, to be active *in itself* and not in the transformation of substance, it must draw back and emerge, as it were, from the 'flood waters' of the organism. In thinking, the organism becomes relatively unimportant, for in the nerves the powerful forces of metabolism are inactive; here the soul disengages itself, detaches itself, and uses the organism as a kind of mirror. For just as each sensory organ reflects a part of the world, so the brain is the inner mirror of the soul. Here the soul creates without matter, without physically moving the convolutions of the brain. Convolutions change only during embryonic development, when the brain is being formed. Later, the cerebral convolutions are frozen solid, as it were, and the soul has disengaged itself. This, indeed, is why the brain seems so inert: it has had to give up many life processes in order to set the soul free. Thus afraid of too great a submersion in bodily processes, the soul recognizes its reflection in the brain and becomes conscious. This recognition corresponds to what the swimmer discovers when he emerges from the waters and climbs on to the shore. He thinks to himself, 'I was in there.' And suddenly he notices that he can see himself in the surface of the water. He is no longer aware of the water's appearance, but only of his own reflection. He forgets the water in the process.

When the soul is engaged in feeling, it is something like a swimmer who is neither submerged nor on dry land, but who is swimming: he lifts his head, makes rhythmic movements in order not to sink, submerges a little and again emerges to the same degree. This is how the soul behaves in the heart and lungs. It is active, it accomplishes something, it immerses itself and then emerges again. And thus, rhythmically maintaining a balance between 'above' and 'below'—as the swimmer must always do—through the marvellous activity of respiration and circulation, the soul experiences itself in feeling. Heartbeat and pulse are the rhythmic waves of the soul as it 'swims' in the forces of the blood.

If we take in this picture we shall understand, not abstractly but graphically, the great polarities at work in man and how they can be reconciled. We shall recognize that while each of the organs has its unique task, because they are grouped in a harmony of three systems all can work together to make a whole. When all three bodily systems are in harmony, man's being of soul and spirit has a healthy and serviceable instrument. Rudolf Steiner once summed up the idea of the threefold human organism in the following meditative saying:

> In the heart weaves feeling,
> In the head shines thinking,
> In the limbs lives strengthening will.

> Light that is weaving,
> Weaving that strengthens,
> Strength that gives light:

> That is man.

Chapter Two

THE HEART—ORGAN OF THE HEART QUALITY

We shall now concern ourselves with the organ in man that is the centre of his life, one of his most important organs—the heart. Much has already been said about this organ and many studies have been made, but it is only relatively recently that we have gained a clear idea, in one sense, of the function of the heart and its part in the total blood circulation. It was not until the beginning of modern history that the Englishman, William Harvey, discovered that the blood does not flow in arbitrary fashion in the arteries and veins, but that it moves in a circular path. The concept of circulation connected with the heart really made its first appearance at that time. Prior to that, it was already known that the blood flows from the heart to the lungs and back again; we still speak today of the pulmonary circulation. Blood which has been oxygenated in the lungs and has returned to the heart then flows via the arteries to all the organs, to every part of the human organism, returning again via the veins, those blood vessels which often appear bluish beneath the skin. Blood flows back to the heart from two sides, collecting in the upper and the lower *vena cava*.

The heart is divided into sections; it is a hollow muscle with subdivisions in it: we are referring, of course, to the cardiac chambers. There are four such chambers (see Figure 2, right and left auricles, and right and left ventricles) with their corresponding openings. Between the auricle and the ventricle there is an opening, both on the right and on the left

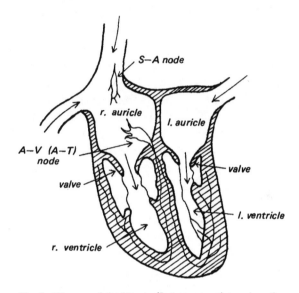

Fig. 2. Diagram of the Heart. (Pulmonary valve and aortic valve not shown.)

side of the heart. On each side, at the point where the ventricle joins a vessel (the pulmonary artery or the aorta), we again find something special, the so-called cardiac valves. Much thought has been devoted to these valves, which have been closely examined in heart specimens. It has been noted that these valves are constructed to allow blood to flow in only one direction, so that it is justifiable to say that they function like mechanical valves. Such valves can be found on many different types of pump, in which a current—usually of water—is subjected to pressure, with the end result that this liquid can move in only one direction. So a valve is something which allows passage in one direction only, as in the inner tube of a bicycle, which has a valve through which air must enter. The trick is that it cannot escape again. Of course, a bicycle valve has a completely different structure from that of a cardiac valve, but its functions are the same. Blood is supposed to flow from the auricle into the ventricle but not vice versa; otherwise the whole heart, the whole circulation, indeed, the whole man would be thrown into a state of chaos.

The details of the construction of the cardiac valves are not so important at the moment. You might picture them as small doors that open in one direction so that the blood can flow through. Of course, after the tired blood has developed new force and drive in the ventricle, it would flow back into the auricle if this ingenious valve did not close so that the blood can continue flowing in one direction only. As we said, there are four such valves in the heart: at the juncture between the auricle and the ventricle on both sides of the heart, and at the opening leading from each ventricle.

Man was so advanced in the seventeenth century that he was fully able to comprehend a mechanical phenomenon such as this. No Greek or Egyptian, for example, ever understood anything about cardiac or mechanical valves, although it is quite possible that they, too, undertook closer examinations of animal hearts. Not until the seventeenth century could one speak of a flowing system and of the fact that the blood was subjected to pressure in the heart, exerting far more force when it left the heart than when it entered the right auricle. Finally, the idea evolved of the heart as nothing more than a pump—a pump which, like an ordinary water pump, must distribute and subject a liquid which comes from some source to pressure, so that it continues to flow in one specific direction, no longer affected by gravity. In this way, water can be pumped to the top floor of a building that is located higher than the water source itself. We can also view the great mystery of the blood's flowing in all directions within us in this way—it also flows 'uphill' to the head, for example. If you stand on your head, your blood is hardly affected, for it then simply flows uphill to the feet. Your face gets red in this position because somewhat more blood than normal congests in the head, but such congestion is for the most part corrected. When you are standing, blood flows upwards from the legs for possibly more than a metre and then returns to the heart, although it can certainly become congested in the legs quite easily. This is common knowledge to anyone who has observed his own or someone else's varicose veins, in which the blood is in danger of succumbing to the force of gravity and sinking. In many heart diseases, the circulation characteristically no longer functions in the proper way so that gravity, which is an integral part of us, begins to affect it, causing blood to be left behind. The blood then extravasates, resulting in oedema, so-called 'water-legs'. In the process, litres of fluid may remain in the tissue, causing serious illness, of course.

The view of the heart as a pump did not remain an isolated one. For in the end the liver came to be viewed solely as a kind of chemical laboratory, though a magnificent one, just like the stomach, where it was determined that hydrochloric acid and other substances effect a purely chemical breakdown of the foodstuffs. The walls of the stomach also help to grind up the food to some extent. So man gradually learned to perceive all the organs in a fully mechanical and materialistic way, solely from the chemical or physical point of view. In this view, the lung is a bellows, and the transfer point for air, oxygen, and carbon dioxide. Air is forced out under pressure if it is not needed and sucked in again because of a partial vacuum that can even be measured in the expanding chest cavity. The muscles were viewed as a power engine with a system of levers. From head to foot man could really be explained in more or less mechanical terms as a completely understandable, though complex, piece of equipment.

Only in the case of the head was the situation more difficult. I have already shown how the head was viewed as the exclusive seat of the soul, because it does indeed play a major role in the origination of our conscious activity of ideation. Although the eye was believed to be comparable to a piece of photographic equipment, the brain and nerves remained the only part of the body not viewed solely in mechanical terms because they were thought to be permeated by the soul. This situation, however, did not last long. At the end of the last century, when materialism in many respects entered its first great golden age, numerous doctors, especially physiologists and psychiatrists, were already of the opinion that the brain secretes thoughts the way the liver does gall. According to this view, man's soul and his life of spirit were not something independent, but rather a product of specific chemical processes in the brain and, like them, transitory. It seemed only a question of time before it could be ascertained which chemical formula of the 'changing molecular arrangements' fitted 'freedom', 'divinity', or 'immortality' into a specific cerebral convolution.

In the end, the entire human being became a chemical laboratory and a machine: by the first half of the eighteenth century a Frenchman, La Mettrie, had already written a book entitled *L'homme machine* (Man as Machine). So we see that in considering the heart, we are touching upon an essential part of the total conception and view of man. We must ask the question, 'Can we—dare we—really view it as a machine, as a pump?' This question is not so easy to answer, for we have seen that it does make sense to speak of valve functions, of pressure systems, of circulating fluid, and so forth, in this connection. And yet there is something in every simple soul—or should I say, in everyone with common sense— which resists the idea of viewing such an organ, which is at the very least the centre of our life, as a pure mechanism.*

We have already seen that the whole human being, from head to foot, is the expression of his soul-life. There is no organ system which does not help to bear and to manifest the soul, in order to serve as an instrument for our soul-life. Earlier we spoke about the life of the soul in man being divided into the three basic functions of ideation, feeling, and willing. We then enlarged upon the way in which the head with its sense organs, nerves, and brain serves to present the ideas, the images that make up our consciousness, which we remember, and which we move around and reflect on. The sense organs and the brain have purely reflecting functions in this activity. We said, however, that when we want to translate an idea, an image, into reality through a deed, through the will, then we need our limbs. The will and the forces of the will in man are manifested in the limbs, where, in addition to the bones, tendons, and joints, the most important organ for realizing the human will is the muscles. We

* The important observations and experiments of the Polish heart surgeon, Dr. Leon Manteuffel-Szoege, give direct evidence that the pump-analogy for the action of the heart is both misleading and incomplete. This work is published as a series of articles in *The British Homeopathic Journal*, Vol. LVIII: No. 3, July 1969; No. 4, October 1969; Vol. LIX: No. 1, January 1970.—Ed.

saw how during metabolism in the stomach and intestine—where there are also muscles—unconscious processes of the will are at work deep inside man, transforming substances there just as man can consciously will to transform them outside with his hands. But most important was our search for the functions and organs that serve as the basis or bearer of human feeling, in other words, of what we experience when we are in a gay or listless, happy or sad mood, when we feel sympathy or antipathy. We then described what lies between the head and the limb system: the rhythmic functions that are manifested particularly in respiration, blood circulation, and heartbeat. All these rhythmic functions form the basis, in their contraction and expansion, in their oscillations, in their whole rhythmic movement, for what oscillates in man's soul between desire and aversion, sympathy and antipathy, love and hate, or whatever we want to call it.

I want you to have the sketch of the human being with his threefold nature once more in front of you—with his sensory-nervous system as the mirror of his activity of ideation, with his metabolic-limb system as the basis of his willing, with his rhythmic system as the basis of his feeling. In anatomical and physiological terms we spoke of man with his threefold nature as being the instrument of his soul manifesting itself in three ways. Only against this background, keeping the whole man in mind, can we venture to understand a part of man, the heart. Goethe has already taught us that any part of an organism always contains the whole within itself, and that it must be developed from the idea of the whole. Goethe observed this truth in those plants that can generate a whole plant from a small piece cut off from a leaf. In a way, the ideal goal of our observations would be to bring forth the whole man from correct observation of the heart, and vice versa, just as the human being as a whole brings forth the heart. This will now be our task.

*

Let us return to what we know about the heart itself. The heart is a muscle, so it is composed, roughly speaking, of flesh. It is also red and, like every muscle, contracts and becomes harder, then expands again and becomes softer. We can observe this movement, this activity of the heart, in the pulse. Without a doubt, then, the heart acts like a muscle. What does that mean for us? It means that the heart displays a certain activity; this activity is connected with the fact that matter is in motion or is set in motion in the heart. We have seen that wherever muscles are active, matter is transformed, is activated—in terms of the soul, the activity of man's will is manifested. I have already pointed out that willing does not cease when the mouthful of food is swallowed. Everyone has the feeling that he is willing something when he really chews or when he cracks open a nut. However, as I described earlier, when the mouthful of food is swallowed, our conscious will, or the will which is directed by our consciousness, ceases, and everything further takes place of its own accord. But we had to put this 'of its own accord' in quotation marks, because nothing in this world takes place of its own accord. Even the oesophagus has to work to get the foodstuffs down into the stomach. They do not slide down 'of their own accord', for they also 'slide down' if you stand on your head, because they are actively pushed along by the action of the muscular walls of the oesophagus. The stomach and the other organs also do their jobs the same active way. So we have become familiar with the unconscious work of the soul, the difficulty here being discovering the soul as something alive and at work even if this activity does not appear as conscious soul-life.

The theory of the unconscious plays a great part in modern psychology. And so it is with the heart: it does its job without our consciously willing it. However, it does have a will. It has a really 'hearty' will, which is the source of its activity and energy. So we can say that, in so far as it has heart muscle, the heart manifests itself in the process of willing—it shares in the forces, in the relationships, which affect the limb and metabolic systems in man. We shall not go into the structural details of the heart muscle components at this time. But we can say that the main activity of the will and the main mass of muscle are located in the two large ventricles of the heart, and that of these two, the left ventricle is the most active, the one which manifests the most will. For this reason it also has the thickest muscle. From the point of view of their contents, the ventricles are not larger than the auricles; exactly as much blood enters the auricles as enters the ventricles—otherwise, everything would be thrown into confusion. But the latter are larger because their muscles are thicker and more powerful. So you see that there is a part of the heart where the mass of muscle and muscular activity receive special emphasis, where the heart is particularly an organ of willing.

But the heart also shares in everything the head does. What does the head do? The head is there to observe the world and man himself. To observe the world it has sense organs. (We shall pursue this theme in more detail in Chapter Four.) In order for our soul to be able to take in what we have perceived, a 'wire'—the nerve—extends from each sense organ to the brain. The nerve organs are concentrated there, forming a real 'central control', which we call the central nervous system, where consciousness originates. The head brings what is going on in the outer world and in our own body and soul to consciousness. It gives us a reflection of all of that. Its task is to form a picture of man and of the world for itself. The heart also has this ability to form a picture of man—in certain respects, even of the world—for itself. Moreover, the heart attaches great importance to this ability, developing something like a 'private nervous system', so to speak, for itself. This you can learn from the head: if you want to know about something and want to form a picture of it, you need a nervous system, you need sense organs. And so we see that the heart is willing to sacrifice some of its muscles. The heart is so versatile and skilful that it can do this by transforming some of its muscles into nerves. Interestingly enough, this process of nerve formation begins in the right auricle, in the chamber where all the blood in the body first reaches the heart. At this point, the heart would immediately like to form a picture for itself of what is going on in the blood and begins to form a small piece of brain (see Figure 2, nodes). There are several such ganglia in the heart. One of these small 'brain nodes' is called the Aschoff-Tawara node,* after the famous pathologist, Aschoff, who was my teacher, and the Japanese, Tawara, who, together with him, devoted special study to the cardiac nervous system and discovered this node only a few decades ago.

We see that starting at this point, the heart is indeed completely interwoven in marvellous fashion with nerve fibres that join with nerves from the rest of the organism. Wherever there are nerves, there are also nerve endings, and nerve endings are always sensitive: they sense, feel, taste, and smell something.† So you must picture the heart not only as an actively functioning organ that performs its task mechanically, but as an organ that very carefully

* More commonly known as the auriculo-ventricular node (A–V node).

† Here we are starting from Rudolf Steiner's basic indication that the so-called motor nerves also have sensory functions that 'serve the inner perception of that metabolic process which is the basis of all willing'. See R. Steiner *Von Seelenrätseln* (Riddles of the Soul), Rudolf Steiner Nachlassverwaltung, Dornach, 1960.

observes what is taking place. It is an inwardly attentive organ, one that keeps a watchful eye on itself. In this respect it is a sense organ.* When you reach into a sandbox and feel the sand with your hand, letting it sift through your fingers, you feel whether it is heavy, whether it is dry, whether it is fine or coarse, whether it is freezing cold or pleasantly warm. Just as you feel all these things, so when the heart receives blood and contracts, you can picture it taking hold of the blood in this grasp of contraction. In the process it examines the inner makeup of the blood, including its rate of movement. This examination is very interesting for the heart because the blood is coming from all parts of the body. A very large amount of blood comes from the liver, another large amount comes more from the head, still a third comes from the limbs or the kidneys. You see, the heart tries to learn what is going on throughout the body, what the blood has to report. For example, the heart notices quite clearly that the blood coming from the liver, from the whole lower part of the body above the lower vena cava, feels warmer, and actually is warmer, than the blood coming from the head. Blood from this area is cooler. This temperature difference has, in fact, been measured by scientists, who have thus been put on the

---

* The notion of the heart as a sense organ, found in the writings of Aristotle and St. Thomas Aquinas, was firmly subscribed to by Rudolf Steiner. A summary of these views is provided in H. H. Schöffler's *Die Zeitgestalt des Herzens*, Verlag Freies Geistesleben, Stuttgart, 1975. Recent cardiac research has provided experimental evidence in support of the sensory function of the heart.—Ed.

track of something which otherwise only the heart knows.

Here is another example of the heart's alertness: If you climb four or five flights of stairs quickly, you will suddenly notice you are taking deeper breaths. If you observe yourself more closely, you will notice your heart is beating faster. Why must your blood circulate faster? Because your legs are in motion. The leg muscles need oxygen, i.e., the blood must deliver more oxygen, so the heart must work faster to comply with this need. It knows right away, 'Aha, now the legs are in motion and the blood has less oxygen; I must see to it that the lungs help out here—otherwise, the legs will suffocate.' The heart then beats faster and breathing becomes deeper. The heart is activated in proportion to the activity of the legs or of the whole body. This process does not, however, take place of its own accord, for the heart has noticed that the composition of the blood in the legs is no longer correct. The legs would suffocate and you would get excruciating pains if the blood did not comply properly with the act of will involved in walking. There are also diseases in which the vessels in the legs become so narrow that the person afflicted must stop on account of the pain and wait until the blood has flowed far enough so that he can walk again. This is called intermittent claudication and is a specific condition of impairment of the blood vessels in the legs.

The fact that the heart beats faster when the body

performs physical work shows us that the heart has been paying attention and has adapted itself to the soul's interaction with the body at that moment. As soon as you sit down quietly at your desk, however, you will notice that your heart is beating more slowly, calming down, because the will itself is only minimally active in guiding a pen or doing something similar. The heart is thus a sense organ for the circulation.

In order to be able to observe something, it is always a good idea to have it before you in peace and quiet. When a car races by down a main street at 120 kilometres an hour it is difficult to note the licence number quickly, to see how many people were in it, or whether the driver was smoking, and so forth. There is nothing to it, however, when the car stops. You can determine the licence number and get a good look at everything. The car can then drive on. It is truly one of the mysteries of this world that when you want to observe something, you need peace and quiet for your observations, and that the less something moves, the better you can observe it. Let us also make it clear once more that our sense organs are mirrors and that our brain, as we have already said, is also a magnificent magic mirror through which we form an image of the world and of ourselves. A mirror functions only if it has as smooth and still a surface as possible. We can take the surface of the water as an example. So long as the water has any movement of its own, such as fine ripples or waves, you see the play of the waves and not your own image. You get an ideal, undistorted image only when the surface of the water has become absolutely smooth. For this reason I also explained earlier that you can understand the soul in the brain if you imagine a swimmer coming out of the water and then seeing himself in the still water that he is no longer setting in motion. Stillness, holding up, and stopping are thus bound up with the sensory-nervous system, the formation of a mirror, and the origination of consciousness.

We have seen that many things are brought to a stop in the brain, even the power of regeneration; all movement of the cerebral convolutions is also brought to a stop. Earlier we called the brain an inactive organ, as seen from the outside, and noticed only then that the brain's activity lies in a totally different sphere. This is also true of the heart. Here, too, the heart must take a lesson from the brain if it wants to observe, if it wants to know what is going on in the blood, and if it wants to form a picture of what is going on throughout the body —whether, for example, the body is growing cold.

In order to be attentive, in order to observe in this fashion, the heart needs, in spite of all its activity and movement, an element of stillness and the capacity to hold up and stop. So it copies the example of the head. *The heart is the magnificent organ that brings the blood to a standstill.* Nowhere else in the body of a healthy person is the constantly circulating, flowing, life-stimulating blood allowed to come to a standstill. It may do so only in the heart. In order to do this, the heart has created something that is the opposite of the activity of the red muscle—the cardiac valves, which close, acting as barriers, and hold up the blood. When the blood from above and from below flows together into the right auricle, it is really surprised: at this point it can go no further! This closure does not last very long, of course, but it is decisive—here the blood is stopped for the first time. You can compare this being stopped to what happens when you come to the border between two countries, for instance when you enter Switzerland: customs, a halt, a stop. But you are in a hurry. Why are you being detained, why are you being stopped, why do you have to lose time in spite of the fact that you are travelling by express train? Because this area called Switzerland has placed 'sense organs', its guards, on its border, because it wants to know what is coming in, how it looks, whether anything is being smuggled in, and so forth. As I said before, whenever you want to observe something, you must hold things up. When you have finished your observations, you let things continue again. This is exactly the way the heart acts. I do not mean that it is a big customs office—the blood does not have passports, after all—but the blood might want to smuggle something in which does not really belong there. Here the heart must be attentive by holding up the blood and calling to it four times: 'Stop, stop, stop, stop!' This is the deeper significance of the cardiac valves.

Even in their appearance, these cardiac valves

occupy a position midway between nerve and bone. They are quite fibrous, hard, bloodless, and without muscles. There are even certain animals in which the fibrous sheet of connective tissue in which the valves are anchored has actually hardened into a bone. Just as nature always reveals her secret somewhere, she shows us here, too, that the heart has the courage to take into itself the processes of ossification, of holding up, and of becoming rigid, which are so extraordinarily developed in the brain. In the head all the bones are interlocked (there are no more joints), and the cerebral convolutions are rigid and motionless. Here the element of motionlessness and rigidity, which culminates in ossification, predominates. You must see this connection: the heart has a nerve system and bloodless organs like these valves, which are very sensitive. Perhaps this could be represented in our drawing by a cross, which we can take as an expression of the forces which are at work in the heart, giving it a certain solidity, a certain hardness, and the strength to hold up but also the ability to reject something. For example, when the blood has been in the lungs, in the pulmonary circulation, and then flows back into the left auricle, it is held up again and rechecked to see whether its colour is right, whether it has been properly renewed, whether the air in which the lungs have to breathe is clean, and so forth. The heart notices all these things and says, 'Yes, everything is in order.' Then , after being held up once more in the left ventricle, the blood is allowed to continue flowing through the aorta to the whole body, refreshing and invigorating us.

*

You are now familiar with the heart as a sense organ and with its part in the sensory-nervous system. It is an organ capable of forming a picture for itself of the movement and make-up of the blood. So you see, it has a share in one pole of man, in his activity of ideation, as well as in the opposite pole, in his activity of will, in the metabolic-limb processes.

But if we now ask what the fundamental force of the heart really is, we have to answer: rhythm. It is this potential ability to balance the scales, to harmonize, to look in two directions between contraction and expansion. Just think: the heart must bring the blood to a stop, and the blood is then set in motion again in the heart. The heart must keep stillness and motion in balance. The blood flows in—there is a steady supply; the body needs blood again—there is a steady demand. The heart must keep supply and demand in equilibrium. When the body needs more blood, the heart has to make sure that the blood speeds up accordingly and flows to the body in greater quantity. There is a certain heaviness to the blood—it wants to sink. But the heart is the place where the blood receives the necessary upward thrust again. The heart must keep heaviness and upward thrust in equilibrium. The heart even works as a unit with two different halves, for it actually consists of 'two hearts'. There is really a right heart, which functions fully independently, is joined to the venous circulation, and sends the blood to the lungs, and a left heart. The latter could perhaps be separated from the former and located at a completely different place in the left side of the chest cavity—it should be able to function there, too. The two hearts work together unceasingly and form a higher unity. Thus right and left are continually brought into balance. So far as the systemic circulation is concerned, the heart is in touch with all the organs, with man's whole inner organic world. In the pulmonary circulation, on the contrary, where the heart collects all the blood and sends it to the lungs, it is in contact with the outer world. Here the blood comes in contact with the atmosphere, i.e., with the outer world in the form of air. Once again it must keep the inside—the organs of the body and the blood's experiences there—and the outside—the lungs, which yield themselves up to the outer world—in equilibrium. The heart must be in the middle everywhere, creating harmony between left and right, between above and below, between inside and outside. In order to be able to do this, the heart must be something like a musician, one could say. For how could it create harmony without being musical? It must have a highly developed power of empathy. And there is, in fact, a third fundamental force of our unconscious activity of soul, the one from which the heart lives: the power of feeling.

When you observe something with interest and love, then you have a specific attitude of soul. In order to reflect something, you need only cold reason and your brain. But in order to observe something carefully, with interest and devotion, you need the balance achieved through the soul's power of feeling, of interest, of being able to open up. The heart has a share in this capacity to open up, to feel. This gives the heart its receptivity with respect to the blood from the entire body; it develops a kind of devotion to everything that flows into it. But on the other hand, .the heart also needs something of the soul-force we allude to when we call a person courageous. In order to fulfil its tasks, the heart needs not only a force which sets to work with the heart muscle in accordance with the will, but also one that really goes at its work with courage—one could almost say, that does its work with a certain enthusiasm. And in fact, the heart works with a large, nearly inexhaustible supply of courage for life. You may say, 'How do you know the heart has such courage for life?' We notice this courage through its opposite, just as we really only think about sunshine when the sun has been eclipsed. In the same way, we can tell something about the heart when it is diseased. When it no longer functions correctly, it can frighten a person terribly. As soon as the heart can no longer keep up with its work for some specific reason, tightness and fear arise in the heart—angina pectoris. In a bad attack, this disease causes excruciating pain and a fear of death arising from the heart which overcomes a person—a fear which cannot be combated by anything in the soul. Words of comfort or reassurance are of no avail. Nothing is of any use except giving an injection to relax the muscle and helping the heart directly. It is an unimaginable fear, which the person who has experienced it describes as an abyss. This description is understandable, for the heart, or the human being, senses that if this condition continues, it will be all over for him in a few minutes. It is the abyss of death that the heart senses; that is why it develops such a feeling of fear.

An organ that can radiate such a feeling of fear normally also possesses the opposite force, of course, only we do not notice it. Its primal force is courage for life. In the Middle Ages, when the brave King Richard was dubbed 'the Lionhearted', such things were still known. The heart functions through this oscillation between devotion on the one hand and courageous activity on the other; the heart has a share in the soul-force of human feeling. *A whole man is in the heart*! In so far as it has muscles and manifests will, it has a share in the limb system. But in so far as it slows down and stops the blood, observing and feeling it with its nerve processes in order to form a picture for itself, it has a share in the nervous system and its soul processes. And then, as a rhythmic organ creating a balance, it has a share in the soul-forces of feeling.

For all these reasons it is out of the question to speak of the heart as a pump. It is a living organ, imbued with powerful harmony; and it is still more than that—it is permeated through and through with the soul. Just as piano wires begin to vibrate in sympathy when a human voice sounds, so the heart experiences everything that goes on in the soul. It leaps for joy, it beats faster in expectation, or stands still in fright. In all its moods, the feeling soul needs the heart with its rhythm of circulation and respiration as a physical basis, just as the harmonics need the corresponding key-note.

Because the soul-force of the heart is, of course, an essential part of our whole soul, it is important to ask how each person develops his soul. Is he more attuned to his head, is he prepared to reflect the world coldly and soberly, analysing and dissecting it? Or does he feel the roots of his soul more in his heart, is he more emotionally attuned to his soul's life in his heart and its formative influence on it? We can certainly judge a person according to whether he is more open-hearted or 'closed-hearted', whether he is oriented more towards the side of the heart that holds up the blood and checks everything carefully, or whether he is oriented more towards the side of the heart that is prepared to receive everything and to give it away again with enthusiasm. The important thing is to maintain the right balance between the necessary 'closed-heartedness' that one sometimes needs in life, and too much big-heartedness and open-heartedness. Just as the heart feels the difference between the warmer blood from below and the cooler blood from above, just as it is an organ which fires the whole organism, so must each person ask himself, 'Am I really a cold-hearted or a warm-hearted person? Is my enthusiasm kindled with great difficulty, or perhaps too easily?' We think of some people as being sentimental or soft-hearted, perhaps even cowardly. Or we say that someone has a stone for a heart in his breast, that he is a hard-hearted fellow; the opposite of too much sentimentality is cruelty. The ideal thing would be if we were as harmoniously well-balanced in our souls between above and below as is the healthy heart. But which of us can keep attentive devotion to the world and courageous activity in equlibrium when it comes to working, as the heart does? There are very few such people. But in speaking of such a person, we could not speak of an open or 'closed'-hearted, of a hard or a soft-hearted person. We could only say that he is all heart, that he is a person who receives and observes everything in a heartfelt manner, who has a heart for everything, not only in theory, but also in practice, when it comes to helping by boldly setting to work. In a certain respect one could say that this is the ideal man. Whoever keeps warm-hearted openness and bold setting to work in equilibrium will always find the golden mean in life as a human being through the strength of a sunny disposition. This person is healthy in soul.

*

Of course, the heart, being located in the tension field of the entire human organism, is always in danger of becoming diseased—not because of its own magnificent nature, but because of the way the head overtaxes it through the effects of disordered sensory impressions, of exaggerated attentiveness, and of coldness of emotions; or because of the way the limbs overtax it through exaggerated achievement and haste; but perhaps also because of the way the blood overtaxes it through an excess of ignoble impulses and passions, which also trouble the heart. Most harmful to it, however, are strong emotions. When a person pounds his fist on the table in anger, his heart has to experience it all. The heart has to pay the price when we want to 'boil over' in rage or become rigid with fear. It immediately has to beat faster or slower and to follow the circulation of the blood when we become red in the face. The heart observes everything, experiences everything. On the other hand, the heart's unconscious soul-force grows weak in the long run if it finds no echo in a disposition which is fostered by devotion to, and love and enthusiasm for, true ideals in life. If, in addition, our life does not follow a rhythm or we simply have to act in a disharmonious way because the circumstances of contemporary civilization and of our job demand it of us, then even the best heart will eventually fail. What is cold-hearted in the soul then becomes closed-hearted and hard-hearted in the heart; the heart tenses up, its vessels constrict, and in the end it becomes calcified. It dies inside, so to speak. If, however, it is overtaxed by the metabolism—for example, by the liver, because the person involved eats or drinks too much—then the heart gradually becomes 'soft', it enlarges or suffers fatty degeneration and can no longer retain its shape. Instead of becoming petrified, it threatens to dissolve. Then more of the inflammatory type of diseases appear—for example, an inflammation of the cardiac muscle, where the danger of an enlargement of the heart is always present. A kind of organic big-heartedness comes into being, just as angina pectoris, constriction of the vessels, is an organic closed-heartedness and hard-heartedness.

If it goes so far that the heart can no longer maintain a balance and is assaulted by either of the poles in man, then we must have recourse to wise Mother Nature, who then in her purity yields from the whole cosmos the world of plants. Energy reserves created from the rhythm of the worlds are to be found there, some of which we can then pass on to the heart: forces to invigorate and warm it if it is becoming too hard and narrow. The physician's job is to observe the heart then and to take the right substance from nature. He can do this only if the heart has taught him to observe nature in a heartfelt way; he can in turn administer the right medication only if there are people who process the products of nature with the right interest, the right bold setting to work, so that the physician has suitable medication to administer to the ailing heart. In this way, processers of medicinal substances and doctors work together like a many-chambered heart, mediating between the sick person and healthy nature. Let us hope that their co-operation will become increasingly heartier and more heartfelt in the future.

Chapter Three
METABOLISM AND THE WILL

In the preceding chapters we have traced the co-operative relationship between man's soul and body, and tried to show how the body, in the threefold differentiation of its organ systems, serves as the instrument of the soul. When we try to form a picture of the world or of ourselves, we depend on the sensory-nervous system, which makes possible our perceptions and ideas. This system, as we have seen, functions much like a mirror. Oscillations in feeling, on the other hand, are active in the rhythmic processes, which come together in the heartbeat and respiration to form a special rhythmic system. And finally, the will is manifested in the limbs and metabolic organs, so that we may speak of a metabolic-limb system. It is the latter that we shall now discuss.

With our will we move not only our own body but any object in the environment that we wish to take hold of or change. In the case of our own body, we may straighten our torso; bend or stretch our arms; close or open our hands; or stand, walk, run, or jump. All these varied bodily movements are prerequisite to our ability to move the materials and objects of the world around us. The *muscles* are the focal point for the translation of our will into deed: in them the will manifests itself and directs its activity towards the outer world.

Every visible external movement is preceded by an internal movement of the muscles, which may harden in contraction or relax. An internal shaping of the muscles corresponds to every external form.

Whenever a person works unusually hard or quickly—or even if he must run for a while instead of walking—his body temperature rises; he may even feel hot and start to perspire. If we were to measure this person's temperature without knowing that he had been so active beforehand, we should have to assume that he had a fever.

This overheating is not, of course, a real fever; it passes quickly, and the organism swiftly adjusts itself. But it does show us that *warmth* and the processes related to it are the portals through which the soul can take hold of the world and the body through willing. If our arms and hands are numb with cold, they cannot serve the delicate play of will-forces involved, for example, in the performing of music or in writing. Through warmth we take hold of the body in such a way that our soul can appear as 'willing' soul. In this process real combustion takes place in the muscles. This combustion clears the way for the soul into matter, and at the same time, releases for the soul itself the energies that make physical strength possible.

We can easily understand that warmth is indispensable to the manifestation of will—that is, taking hold of matter, or working—for if we pursue this premise, we see that heat can expand and melt all substances, set them in motion, bind them together, and alter them profoundly. And we have yet another indication that the will is connected with fire, for we think of the choleric, who is without doubt very will-oriented, as having a fiery temperament. And when a person is unable to control his will and pounds his fist on the table, we say that he is boiling over with anger, or that he is burning with rage. And it may be just as well to have such hotheads around, since they show us how closely the will is connected with heat and fire!

To make this connection, the will must make use of the limbs, and on a more complex level, even of the miraculous preparation of substances that are later oxidized (burned) during muscular metabolism. Because it continually extracts, consumes, and internally transforms substances, our organism constantly requires new substance in order to carry forward its life. Our inner organism is thus in constant motion, moving, transporting, kneading, but most important, chemically altering substance, so that it may be used in the processes of life.

All these basic processes are summed up under the term 'metabolism'. Underlying all the metabolic processes in man are delicate, unconscious will forces. Only this hidden power of the will enables a person to transport substances properly within himself and to direct their chemical transformation. And whenever the soul wants to be active outside the head, where it lives only in created images, and to enter external reality, it needs the metabolism. For it is only through this transformation of matter that the soul can find its way not only into its own body but also into the material world, the world of work, the earth.

Let us follow these metabolic pathways for a while. In so doing we shall consider three basic activities: first, that of *nourishment*, or the taking in of substance, and secondly, the *excretion* of wastes. In these two processes we can study the alternation between intake and elimination. Between the two lies the work area of the *conversion* of substance in the body's widely differing organs: their transport, modification, and circulation.

The beginning of metabolism is the process of nourishment, which starts with eating. But eating a piece of bread or a noon-day meal is preceded by what the cook does. It is pleasant to watch a cook baking bread, or in general to watch anyone perform some specific task. For here the will is manifest. And in this visible manifestation of will, we can observe many things that give us insight into actions of the will that remain hidden, and are therefore much more difficult to understand.

Watch, for example, a man who is chopping wood. First of all, he must make sure that a piece of matter, the log he wants to chop, is held securely. Then, taking a firm hold of the axe, he swings it and finally throws the chopped-up wood aside. The will always works in this way, taking hold of substance and ultimately releasing it again. A conversion takes place, a 'chopping-up', so to speak, so that pieces of wood fly around and are scattered; but then the will takes charge again and piles everything up, gathering and ordering it, until the neat arrangement is disturbed once more when someone decides to make a fire with this wood, thus bringing it to its destination in the oven.

Now let us watch the cook who wants to bake a cake in this oven, and who is active in her kitchen. What does she do? She takes the most varied substances; she measures the amount of milk or water she needs; she weighs the flour and sugar; she counts the eggs. We shall see that wherever man has to deal with substance—whether in the outer world or within his own body—quantity, number and weight play a special part. When work is done with these three ordering forces, it becomes purposeful action; only then does work have meaning.

This fact becomes especially clear when the housewife bakes a cake. She mixes the various substances in specific amounts; she moves them, stirs them, kneads the dough, and finally shapes it. Or watch what she does with the egg! She separates the unusable, hard, calcium shell, from the usable; she separates this usable part in turn into egg-white and yolk. These she treats quite differently; the white is whipped and the yolk is beaten, and then they are combined again. All this illustrates how the human soul deals with substance when it is active in willing.

Every action of the will has not only an external aspect, the mechanical processing of substance, but also a moral one that everyone can experience in himself or in his fellow man in a very concrete way. For example, we say that a housewife who works quickly and eagerly at baking is diligent. If she measures and weighs correctly and her cake tastes good, we say she is efficient. But if she does everything slowly or sloppily, we consider her lazy or even slovenly. On the other hand, she may work over-eagerly or hastily because she has her mind on something completely different or because she is pressed for time. In order to employ the will purposefully, we must continually weigh in the balance the opposite dangers of working too slowly or too quickly.

The *whole* man is always involved in his work. We have seen already that both feeling and ideational thinking are also part of the whole man, of the whole human soul. We may assume that when the housewife bakes a birthday cake she bakes it lovingly, or at least that she works carefully or with special interest. It would be terrible if she baked the cake with complete indifference, or if she were irritated, tense, or annoyed. All these things are possible. Or, if she were overtired, she might begin dropping the eggs because under such conditions her will would be too weak to enable her to work in an orderly fashion.

Let us picture once again the wood-cutter. Suppose he hits a real 'knot' with three branches. He hacks away at it without success. He takes one more swing and the axe gets stuck in the wood; he cannot dislodge it. Then he mutters to himself, 'I *must* be able to get it out', and makes furious efforts to do so. Finally he becomes almost obsessed with his task.

Let us suppose that at this point you approach the man and try to explain to him that if he works more slowly and attacks the problem from a different angle, it will surely go better for him. If he is the choleric, or hot-headed type mentioned earlier, he will fly into a rage and you will run the risk of being hit over the head with a piece of wood.

Here we see how the will can be deflected in a particular direction and become too strong; it is then in danger of becoming obstinate. It is important for us to understand that the will must be active in moderation, as it lies always between two extremes. Only if we bear this in mind can we observe vividly and correctly the metabolic processes in man: what the stomach, for example, does with the food we put into it, or even what the liver or blood, on the level of internal organ-functioning, do with these substances.

*

Let us assume that the bread or cake is finished. In baking it, the cook has carefully regulated the oven temperature, making sure that the bread was cooked neither too slowly nor too quickly, so that it has neither burned nor failed to rise. Everything has gone smoothly, since the cook was not only interested, diligent and loving in her baking, but also intelligent and attentive. As I have said before, the whole man is always involved in willing—he must *picture* something and *feel* something in order to be able to *act* in the right way.

If we now eat the bread and turn to the process of nutrition, we see that the will again plays a major role. For in taking the first bite, we take hold of a bit of substance with our mouth, with our teeth. We then set to work on it; chewing, we reduce it to tiny bits. We refine the breaking up of matter begun by the wood-cutter with his axe, or by the housewife when she dices something with a knife or grinds up nuts in a nutgrinder. Our molars and incisors replace the grinder and the knife. Here, in the mouth, the will activity of metabolism begins, served by the masticatory muscles and the most wonderful and versatile of all man's muscles, the tongue. Here again we see that the will acts by taking hold of substance, drawing it in, and then releasing it again by sending it away—in this case by swallowing. Moistened with saliva, the substance is thoroughly kneaded, until it finally takes on a form. Just as the housewife moulds the finished dough, so do we form the mouthful of food and finally send it away shaped as a ball. We swallow!

At this point real metabolic activity begins. From now on, our conscious soul-life has nothing more to do with the digestive process. We cannot consciously do anything nor can we know anything that now takes place unless we study physiology or medicine.

What does happen now? The mouthful of food slides down the oesophagus, or rather, is actively pushed along. For the oesophagus is not simply a tube or pipe that materials slip through; it also has muscle. Just as muscle fibre extends throughout the walls of the stomach and small and large intestines, so the internal wall of the oesophagus is equipped with muscle covered with a smooth layer of skin containing glands.

Just as important as this layer, called the *mucous membrane,* is the muscular structure of the stomach and intestinal system. If we examine these muscle fibres closely, we see that their internal fine structure is quite different from that of the skeletal muscles. For these muscles are smooth, while the skeletal muscles are quite complex and under the microscope reveal a wonderfully rhythmic arrangement. Wherever there are muscles, as we recall, the will is active. Soul-forces similar to those active in the limbs are also in the intestine, but these are soul forces that we cannot control with our conscious activity of ideation, with our head. Thus we speak of *involuntary* movements, removed from the forces of ideation. Yet the fact that this activity is involuntary does not mean that it proceeds somehow by itself, it only appears to do so. In reality, it is an extremely active process, diverse and absolutely precise, that takes place in our internal organs during the subtle transformation of matter.

We can begin to get a feeling for the precision and diversity of this activity in the stomach, an incredibly hardworking organ. Kneading the mouthfuls of food and adding liquid to them, it continues the work of the salivary glands in the mouth, and in a certain sense, even the activity of the cook, who mixes the dry flour with milk, water and eggs, thus liquefying it. The stomach continues all these activities. It mixes together everything it receives, and in a continuation of the breaking down of foodstuffs begun by chewing, it chemically alters the internal fine structure. The chemical alteration and movement of substance that take place in the stomach are only continuations of the coarse, physical-mechanical process that goes on in chewing. Once again there are two basic activities: the seizing and taking in of substance, and the separation and releasing of it. For the stomach takes hold of the substances it receives from the oesophagus, and releases them through the pylorus into the small intestine.

From this point on, the will forces active in digestion become increasingly subtle. The food substance, too, is considerably refined, having been completely liquefied in the stomach. No separate pieces remain; all have been reduced to a homogeneous liquid pulp called *chyme*. The body has already contributed large quantities of its own fluid, its own substance, in order to speed this liquefaction. In the small intestine the chyme is further broken down, both chemically and mechanically. Again and again, through specific movements of the intestine, the chyme is precisely distributed over the intestinal wall. Then, at the next instant, the intestine contracts and collects the diffused substance, forming from it tiny balls like a string of pearls. So it goes, back and forth—contraction, expansion, transport—until the substance has been so processed, so broken down, so decomposed and refined, that it can at last be absorbed by the organism itself through the walls of the intestine.

This process of absorption can no more take place of its own accord than can any other metabolic activity. The substance does not seep passively through the intestinal wall like a liquid through filter paper, or like fresh food leaking through a paper bag. There is no question of that. The nutritive substances are absorbed *actively* by the intestinal wall, just as actively as when we open our mouth to take a bite and in the process use our tongue and teeth.

In the intestine we have thousands upon thousands of tiny 'mouths' and 'tongues' that take hold of substance, taste, and absorb it. In these structures, called *intestinal villi*, tongue and mouth are one. They are as delicate as the tiny filaments of a carpet, so that the inner wall of the intestine looks like a velvet rug. Yet, these millions of fragile tongues are equipped with the finest of muscles; undulating rhythmically, they taste and absorb the chyme that is spread over them, ultimately passing it on, into the blood stream. Only now has the food substance really entered the human organism. Until this point it has been in the cavity of the stomach and intestine, which may be regarded as outer world turned inward.

The polaric, alternating processes we have found are will-activity and also play a part in the small intestine. For example, when someone bites into a cherry, he notices immediately that the stone is too hard to eat, and he spits it out, sending it in the opposite direction from that in which food ought to go. The small intestine, with its villi, functions similarly, not only mixing the substance it receives, but continually separating and dividing it. All the hard, unusable waste materials—for example, the cellulose present in bread or lettuce, most of which we cannot digest—are rejected and transported further; they are not absorbed. A real differentiation takes place. Everything that is separated, eliminated, and transported further in this way then passes into the large intestine, which dries it out, removes the water, and forms the faeces. Thus, even the unusable substance is given shape. In addition, the usable, liquid portion is retained and absorbed. Finally, excretion from the intestine takes place. We have now traced the entire path of digestion in man. All this processing of substance is connected with unconscious activity of the will, but also with dull sensation.

*

We have already mentioned the fact that the will has two sides, the purely physical, and the moral. Let us now consider the moral aspect of this unconscious will activity in the internal organs. We have all experienced the situation in which this unconscious will becomes sluggish, in which the inner will of the organism no longer sets to work in the right way. Becoming lazy, it simply leaves the substances where they lie. We say that the person so afflicted has a sluggish metabolism, by which we usually mean that he is constipated. But what appears in such an obvious way as severe constipation, as obstipation, is something that can subtly affect the entire organism. If this happens we are well on the way to serious metabolic disorders, to real diseases.

As we have seen, the other danger is the will's becoming over-eager and working so quickly and hastily that we can no longer keep track of the situation and let it slip from our grasp, as the egg slips out of the housewife's hand. When this happens in the stomach and intestine, when everything moves too quickly and in too disorderly a fashion, the person affected has the opposite of constipation: diarrhoea. Nourishing substance is again lost, improperly processed, though in this case because the intestine is *over*-active. This over-eagerness, if we wish to call it that, can become as extreme as the case of the woodcutter who could no longer manage the branch that resisted his efforts. Like the woodcutter, the intestine is then no longer able to handle its task, so it overexerts its will and becomes obstinate and cramped.

Let us take a second example. The gall bladder is also a muscular hollow organ that works with liquid substances. First, it absorbs the gall secreted by the liver, stores it, concentrates it, and then secretes it into the intestine as needed. If the metabolism as a whole becomes sluggish and food is not being processed properly, it is possible that the gall's composition will also be affected, so that even more substance is lost to the organism. Biliary gravel or even gall stones may develop at this point.

Since the body always feels obliged to come to grips with matter, the gall bladder tries to handle this foreign body, which is now a stone, by trying to get rid of it; it tries to expel it. We can almost imagine it saying to itself, 'This stone is dead! It doesn't belong in the body, but in the outside world.' So the gall bladder wants to expel the stone, but that is not simple to do. When we spit out a cherry stone, the act of getting rid of the unwanted substance is accomplished quickly. The gall bladder now tries to assert its will in the same way, but its stone gets stuck. At this point the gall bladder becomes exasperated, trying harder and harder until it becomes so over-eager that it is just as obstinately set on its work as the woodcutter whose axe gets stuck in the wood.

This is a very unpleasant situation, for the person in question is having an attack of biliary colic: the gall bladder has become cramped and can no longer relax. The actual significance of a cramp is that the will cannot let go. Outside help must be brought in; the other actions of the will and the rhythm of the blood circulation must be stimulated by adding warmth, in the form of a hot compress, for example, or by diverting the organism in some way. For the organism is paying too much attention to the area of the gall bladder and in the process has become conscious at a point where it is usually fast asleep. This awakening is expressed as pain. In extreme cases, the necessary diversion can be supplied only by administering an anaesthetic, which forces the organism to forget the whole situation completely, at the same time causing it to fall asleep and relax. The gall bladder then releases the stone, just as we let go of a book when we fall asleep while reading.

*

So we see that health and sickness are to the unconscious will as moral and immoral traits of character are to the conscious sphere of human work and will activity. Of course it would be absurd to heap abuse on the gall bladder, applying moral standards to it and saying that it is acting like a choleric, or that it really should behave better. Moral criteria fail here; what matters is whether the organ is healthy or sick. It is important to emphasize this point, for despite the obvious contrast between the moral plane and the plane of health, there is a definite connection between the two. We have already seen this paradox in our observation of the heart.

Such connections become especially clear in eating, since there is in the metabolic system a strong interaction between physiological and moral processes. If, for example, it is a person's nature to eat hurriedly, over-eagerly, bolting down his food, so that someone must finally say to him, 'You know, you really chew your food in a most disorderly and sloppy manner!', his stomach certainly cannot remain unaffected. For the stomach must then take over the work that has not been done properly in the mouth; it has to do extra kneading, breaking down, and moistening. If we continually impose too much work upon someone without good or sufficient reason, he will eventually become irritable and unwilling. We cannot really blame him. But if we cannot blame a person for feeling this way, we should not blame the stomach either when it suddenly becomes irritated, and we have an upset stomach. It is very interesting to look at an upset stomach on an X-ray screen, for we can actually see that it is working over-eagerly—hastily and nervously, in short, that it is cramped.

We can follow the stomach's work, this action of the will, very precisely (see Figure 3). The food enters through the cardiac sphincter; it leaves through the pylorus. The stomach kneads and processes the food by contracting at one point, then relaxing again and contracting at the next point, so that muscular movements ripple over the stomach like waves. While the stomach is completing its activity at the lower end, the next wave is already beginning at the top. The proper term here is *peristalsis*; we speak of peristaltic waves. So when the stomach is upset, when we overtax it by eating too quickly or by eating food that is too hot, it must process everything more thoroughly: it sets to work more vigorously; its entire length becomes constricted, and its contractions more extreme. But at the same time everything happens at a faster rate, and we immediately notice that something is wrong with the stomach. Thus, something we can control if we eat in full awareness is carried over into the unconscious region of the organs; here what we do improperly on the conscious level causes illness.

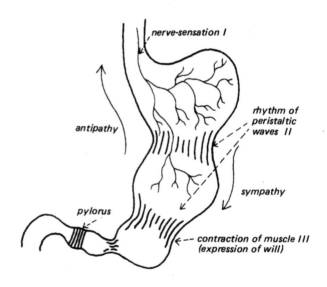

Fig. 3. The Threefold Function of the Stomach

A great number of man's illnesses are caused by the way he lives his life of soul, by the way he thinks, feels and wills—though in many cases this connection is difficult to see, since it is often subtle and indirect, and cause and effect may be separated by many years. Nevertheless, whether a person's thoughts are clear or confused, vivid or abstract, whether his will is firm or weak, all in the long run have a great influence on his health. For *in reality the soul is a unity* despite the contrasts that force us to differentiate between the conscious soul-life and unconscious activities of the soul. We do not have two separate souls in our organism, one taking care of the coarse work of the organs while the other lives at leisure and is active only in the 'upper chamber', of the head. All these things are inwardly connected. The entire soul is always involved when some process is taking place, and this is also true in the stomach. We have seen already how the hardworking housewife is totally involved in her work, not only with her will, but also with her feelings, with the positive feeling of interest or love, of enjoyment of her work. She is likewise paying attention, her senses fully alert, so that she can picture clearly what she is doing. So it is with the stomach; it needs all the soul's activities in order to do its work properly.

We have also seen that rhythmic activity is the basis of feeling. If we now observe the rhythmic waves that ripple across the stomach in regular, seemingly fixed, succession, we begin to understand what a wonderfully rhythmic organ it is (Figure 3, II). And when the pylorus opens and closes, then opens and closes again, this movement too is rhythmic. So the stomach's activity is not just a crude, irregular swirling around of substance—the rhythm itself indicates that forces of unconscious *feeling* must affect its functioning. And this is actually the case. For it could be said that the stomach enjoys its work; it does its work with a kind of pleasure, a kind of sympathy, which, like the heart's courage, can be shown by way of contrast. For the stomach, like the human soul, has its own antipathies. If what you have eaten does not agree with it—if it tastes the food and notices there is something wrong with it, that it is spoiled, that neither the stomach nor the organism can use it—it develops an aversion to it, an antipathy that intensifies until it does the same thing you do with the cherry stone you cannot use. With vehemence, the stomach sends its contents in the opposite direction! A feeling of nausea then becomes obvious to the observer, showing us clearly that even the stomach has something like a soul of its own.

In order to perform any action, the soul must also be attentive and must form a picture of the situation; for this it needs the nervous system, as we have seen. The stomach, of course, is well supplied with nerves, and these are what enable it to be dimly aware of how full it is and of what is in it (Figure 3, I). In this sense, it observes its work and forms a picture of it, and it is extremely important that this picture be accurate.

Thus, even a will-organ like the stomach recapitulates the whole man. Through its muscles, it is active in willing; its rhythmic functioning enables it to experience unconscious, dreamlike feelings of pleasure or aversion. And because it has nerves, it is able to form an inner picture of its work, and to be constantly attentive to what it is doing and to what its task is at that moment. The stomach is a highly sensitive organ.* So we should not picture it simply as a sack or even as a muscular tube in which materials are mechanically kneaded, but we could almost imagine it as a small 'animal' inside us, with all the good characteristics of an animal. We could even say that just as an infant waits eagerly to be fed, the stomach has a kind of desire of its own, and also waits to receive its food. When the infant receives nothing he cries, and when the stomach is not fed, it begins to 'growl', because its desires have not been fulfilled. Imagine a hungry living creature such as a cat, a dog, or even a baby, and picture it as a stomach—only then do you have the right idea of what the stomach is.

Such an organ, like every living creature, can be irritated or upset, diligent or lazy, and can behave in an orderly or sloppy manner. All these things are possible. In the stomach, such sloppiness, or over-fatigue, are manifested in *atony*. It hangs down limply, perhaps even into the pelvis; it no longer does its work properly; and the peristaltic waves are only superficial. Its work is forgotten, the chyme is forgotten, and the person in question suffers from a feeling of fullness. This feeling can be a symptom of very serious illness.

* In connection with these soul forces that form the organs and are bound up in the body, the anthroposophical view of human physiology mentions the 'sentient' body and the organization of astral forces. A trained seer can observe the latter as it lights up in an individual's aura. (See R. Steiner *Theosophy. An Introduction to the Supersensible Knowledge of the World and the Destination of Man.* Rudolf Steiner Press. London. 1973.)

How do we treat such an illness? Let us take this opportunity to express some fundamental thoughts about the efficacy of various remedies. It is well known, for example, that bitters such as gentian are good for the stomach. If we bite into a gentian root and chew up a small piece of it, we make some surprising discoveries. The intense, bitter taste arouses the attention of the tastebuds. The mouth immediately begins to water, that is, glandular activity increases reflexively. The feeling of pleasure aroused by the aromatic spice alternates with a feeling of antipathy towards the bitterness. The latter makes our mouth pucker. We try to swallow the gentian quickly or even to spit it out, thus activating our will to a greater extent than usual. We can well imagine that a limp, atonic stomach would be no more able to react neutrally towards gentian than is the mouth. It is stimulated in every way and contracts, summoning to greater activity the soul-forces that give it form and maintain its nerves, blood vessels and muscles. All this stimulates the circulation of blood and increases the oxygen supply: the stomach is on the road to recovery. We could use a different remedy in a similar fashion to calm an overstimulated stomach.

Neither such a remedy nor the healing process itself should ever be construed as a mere mechanical or lifeless chemical process. Every healing process, even if it takes place in only one specific organ, is concerned with the life and soul-forces of the entire human being. A doctor who recognizes only the chemo-physical effect of a particular medicine is in great danger of assaulting the organism as a whole and might effect a cure of one organ at the expense of other spheres of life. Such a recovery would be only apparent, not real.

*

We have already described how substances pass through the intestinal wall and are absorbed into the organism, into the actual sphere of life. Here the main organ of metabolism is the liver, where countless delicate transformations we cannot even begin to describe take place. Let us single out just one of these transformations, the liver's treatment of the sugar that enters it, through the portal vein, from the intestine. The liver notices that this blood is far too sweet for the organism to use. Having 'tasted' the blood, the liver removes from it the excess sweetness, which it stores in relatively insoluble, liquid form for later use. Just as the woodcutter gathers pieces of wood he has chopped, arranges them into a pile, and says, 'Now there is enough for when it is needed,' so the liver stores up sugar. When a person runs upstairs, for example, then downstairs, and then upstairs again, his body needs sugar, for he is burning sugar, among other things, in his muscles. In order to build themselves up again, the muscles must take sugar from the blood flowing through them. As a result, the blood itself loses sugar, so that the liver must mobilize the substance we call glycogen, dissolve it, separate it, and release it into the blood, through which it is transported to the muscles, where it is needed.

A study of this process offers insights into the most delicate workings of metabolism, for the forces at work here perform the most subtle of the soul's activities of will. The reader may object, 'But I know all about the structure of the liver; it is made up of cells and connective tissue, but has no muscles at all. And you have said that the will manifests itself only where there are muscles.' This is not quite true. As we have seen, the will reaches into the material world through the portal of warmth. Of course, in order to execute powerful acts of will, of strength in the purely physical sense, we need our muscles. But in the blood and internal organs the movements necessary for the transformation of substance become very subtle indeed; to a large degree the only movement that takes place is chemical—the synthesis, breakdown, and mixture of substances—so that mechanical movement becomes totally unnecessary. We could say that the will is active here only in homoeopathic doses.

Consider the different acts of will involved in various occupations. When the forest ranger makes a notch on a tree, for example, to indicate that it must be felled, this is an act of will. But it is crude in comparison with the act of will performed by the engraver when he makes an etching on a copper plate. Yet both are acts of will. Metabolic acts of will, which take place deep within the internal organs, are as delicate as those of the engraver. If we try to lengthen a steel wire by force, stretching it between our two hands, our efforts will be in vain. It will not stretch by even half a millimetre. But if we hold the wire quietly in our hands and let their warmth work on it, it can easily be stretched. Similarly, the will can accomplish through warmth everything necessary for the proper direction of the movement and transformation of substance. If we are to be internally healthy, these subtle will forces (which are related to the blood's impulses and forces of desire) must be active in our liver and in our other metabolic organs.

All these upbuilding, anabolic forces require the proper stimulation and care if they are to sustain our health to an advanced age. Long-term health is not possible if with our food, however small the dosage, we are continually introducing into our bodies chemicals or even poisons, as is increasingly the case in today's mass-produced civilization. Let us take the relatively harmless example of an artificial sweetener. The intense sensation of sweetness released by such a substance seems to announce to the liver that it can refill its sugar depositories. With the inner desire peculiar to the liver, with a hidden appetite, it tastes the intestinal venous blood in question. At this point the liver experiences something like disappointment; it strains to grasp thin air, so to speak, with its organic will. If such a process is repeated many times, a kind of subtle resignation, a kind of paralysis of the instinctive activity of the will develops. The organic life-will of the soul withdraws, neglecting the substances to some extent, so that they are easily lost to the living organism. The foundation is laid for serious metabolic illnesses such as rheumatism and stones.

So even a substance that seems completely harmless in the chemo-physical sense can still have harmful effects in the context of the whole organism. The situation is similar in the case of the inferior food products eaten by Western man today. Even worse, of course, are out-and-out poisons, such as preservatives and toxic insecticides, which directly damage life-forces and cellular activity. Naturally, all these harmful substances must have a combined, cumulative effect in order to bring about a real illness of the kind we have described above.

In the metabolism as a whole, it is of utmost importance that everything proceed correctly, in the right proportions, quantities, and numbers. Here the actions of the will are wonderfully wise (though we usually say 'instinctive') in carrying out great internal work and organization. We have seen that in order to bake a cake or a loaf of bread, attention and love are needed to ensure that the correct amount of sugar is added. In like manner the organism, especially the liver, continually checks to see that the blood has the right degree of sweetness. Other organs help in this process: The pancreas secretes a substance that prevents excessive amounts of sugar from remaining in the blood; and the kidney, functioning via the adrenal gland, secretes into the blood a substance that stimulates the liver to release its sugar. In this way, tasting the sweetness of the blood, the organism weighs precisely and carefully the quantities of sugar it must give to it.

Alas, if fatigue, enervation, or lack of interest affects the action of the will. For in this case the internal organs themselves are affected by sluggish metabolism: substance remains where it is and is no longer under control—a situation far worse than if it remained in the large intestine. For when sugar stays in the organs and blood because the organism can no longer handle it properly, the person affected has diabetes.

To find the cause of such an illness, we must often go back twenty, thirty or forty years and see how the patient's conscious will had been active to cause the unconscious, organic will to become so tired, enervated, and incapable of proper functioning. As we have seen, such failure of will may have many causes.

In closing, let me mention just one of them. Rudolf Steiner has said that if a very young child is given toys that are too sophisticated or mechanized—for example, a doll that has a beautifully painted face, opens and closes its eyes, and says 'Mama'—he only *seems* to enjoy it. Because he cannot use his imagination in playing with such a doll, the child soon becomes bored, and the delicate creative will-forces he naturally seeks to unfold in every imaginative game fail to develop. There is no resonance in the forces of will that build up his organs. Yet a simple, home-made rag doll not only permits the child to add something from his own imagination—a smile or frown, for example—but actually stimulates him to do so. If his imagination is not allowed to work in this way, his unconscious will forces are actually weakened; they too lose interest, so to speak, if the child is bored by his toys. Thus, such boredom and disinterest in childhood can create a physical predisposition to disease in adulthood. The child is so profoundly affected because his soul-forces, unlike the adult's, are still deeply involved with his growing organism and closely bound up with it.

This is why any immoral actions in a child's surroundings are so damaging not only to his soul, but even to his body. A choleric father's bursts of anger can have shock-like effects, obstructing and weakening the life-will that forms the child's organs. In this way, an inherited predisposition towards a relatively harmless weakness in the gall bladder, for example, can be greatly aggravated, and even lead to the formation of gall stones in old age.

Such damage, however, can be countered to a large degree if the child's teacher presents his material with artistic interest and loving enthusiasm. Through the method he uses, the teacher speaks not only to the head and the memory, but to the whole child in his feelings and his will. Teaching to which the child can respond with warmth may tire the head, but at the same time it refreshes and exhilarates the rest of the organism right down to the physical body, counteracting the premature drying up and paralysis of life-forces, and with them the predisposition to many illnesses.

Throughout these observations, I have tried to show that the human being is a *unity*, and that the corporeal and physiological life of his organs is bound up in a hidden way with his conscious life of soul. It is because of this deep connection that we must all turn our attention to the *way* we do our work and live our life of soul. Whenever we do our work carefully, with interest and love, with diligence and attentiveness, there are many positive results, not the least of which is good health.

Chapter Four

THE SENSORY-NERVOUS SYSTEM AS MIRROR OF THE SOUL

When we wake each morning, we open our eyes. Refreshed, we look into the world, using our body, which has rested during the night. But what is the difference between the sleeping and the waking eye, between the eye that is closed, yielding itself to darkness, unseeing, and the eye that opens to the world when we wake? When we wake from sleep, not only sight is restored to us, but also the life of all the other senses, such as hearing, touch, smell and taste. It is our whole conscious life of soul that appears when we wake. So the difference between the sleeping and waking eye is actually part of the larger question we have discussed throughout these lectures: How does man's soul live in his body? At this point let us consider the origin of *conscious* soul-life and its connection with the senses, nerves and brain. We designate all these organs as the sensory-nervous or nerve-sense system.

We know, of course, that the main senses, the superior senses, of sight, smell, hearing, and taste, are concentrated in the head. Nerves radiating from all the sense organs of the body join in the head, where they form, out of their manifold branchings, crossings and interweavings, something extraordinary: the brain. From the head the sensory-nervous system extends to the whole body, reaching every organ, every point on the skin, the smallest toe. We can feel heat, pain, touch, and countless other sensations all over our body. The life of our nerve-sense system, then, although concentrated in the head, extends over the whole body; so not only our eyes open when we wake, but our whole soul opens to the world, throughout the body. How does this awakening take place?

We have already seen that in order to understand the workings of the sensory-nervous system, we must compare it with a mirror. The mirror exists to give us as good, clear, sharp an image of the world as possible; we judge its quality by the clearness of this image. The sense organs are in fact like mirrors and their function, too, is one of reflection. Their task is to give us as accurate an image of the world as possible. Because this function is specially evident in the eye, let us begin here in our attempt to learn about the senses, nerves and brain.

The eye is highly complex and, unlike any other sense organ, it actually has its own small piece of brain. For when the eye develops in the embryo, an inquisitive nerve, so to speak, a tiny piece of brain, grows out from the brain rudiment. At this time, the brain is still mobile; its convolutions are still being formed and it is only beginning to take on a final shape. This inquisitive shoot grows towards the front and opens like a blossom, eventually forming the cup of the eye, a multi-layered part of the brain with genuine brain cells: the *retina*. From the outside, from the skin, tissue grows in towards this cup, invaginates, and ties itself off, forming the *lens*. We can see already how complex the eye is. From the outside something develops inward, from the inside something grows out; the two join and are literally rounded off in the living eyeball.

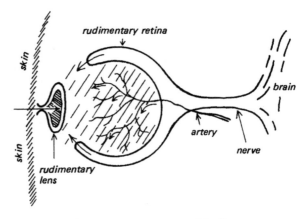

Fig. 4. The Development of the Eye

This goal could never be attained, however, if blood did not flow into the eye, nourishing it, supplying it with oxygen and vitalizing it. Yet the blood cannot remain here; the organism must get rid of it at the right time. For if the whole eye were permeated with blood, as is the case in the embryo (Figure 4, artery), we would either see everything as cloudy red or we would see nothing at all, for the eye would be unable to form proper mirror-images. A mirror must be clear. So after the blood has helped build up the eye, it must recede again, and may only continue its activity in the background, behind the retina, in the choroid membrane. Later we shall see yet another vital role that the blood must play in the finished, functioning eye.

Each of us can experience how the eye gives us an image of the world, furnishing us with mirror-images no matter which way we direct it. But we become especially aware of this mirror function of the eye when we experience a strong impression of light. If, for example, we look directly at the blinding sun, and then somewhere else, we notice that something seems to be wrong with our eyes. If we look at another person's head, we cannot see it. What do we see? An after-image of the sun! Wherever we look, a kind of blackish hole appears; the sun has left something behind in our eyes. The bright sphere of the sun, which the eye takes in and actually reproduces in the retina through the complex functioning of the lens, has left an impression.

We might compare this impression with a hole; just as we file papers in a notebook by punching three holes in them, so each impression of light may be said to punch a hole in the retina. If the impression of light is especially strong, we become aware of this hole; we simply cannot see anything else, because—as strange as this may sound—*all seeing destroys the eye!* Not the whole eye, of course, but a part of it; for in the retina something undergoes catabolism, is actually destroyed. And we know what it is that is destroyed in this way. On the retina, as on a photographic plate, there is a delicate, special layer called the *visual purple*. This substance changes chemically, decomposes, and fades so that an image is formed and retained on the retina.

In this sense we might compare the eye to a camera. A kind of 'negative' of the outside world is formed in the eye. That something is thereby destroyed becomes quite evident when we look at the bright sun and it blinds us. In this extreme case we become aware of the image, the 'hole' that is formed when we look at something. When I look at an audience of about 150 people, I am sure I have 150 holes in my retina. But these are very delicate holes—in homoeopathic doses! You may laugh, but it is true!

Thus each act of seeing is bound up with a catabolic process that is carried into the brain, in a subtle way, through the optic nerves. So the eye that wants to serve the soul must endure having its fine structure destroyed to some extent.

What is the purpose of this catabolic process in the nerves? We can understand it best if we consider it to be a modification of the process we observed in the development of the eye, as a retrogressive metamorphosis of the blood vessels in the vitreous humour. This reversal of metabolic processes, as we have seen, is what makes the clarification of the eye possible, giving the cornea and vitreous humour the transparency, and the lens the crystal-clarity, that allow external light to stream into the darkness of the organism. Thus, on a small scale, the eye is similar to the head, which, as we recall, curbs metabolic processes in order to release the forces of the soul. In a similar way, the process of catabolism creates 'open spaces' in the retina and optic nerve, through which the body's soul-force can slip into the eye from within and meet the outer light. Only in this way can the soul find its way to the objects we perceive, and explore them.

By sacrificing part of its vitality and substance, its visual purple, for example, the eye is raised from the level of an insensitive organ, merely organically alive, to that of a sentient organ, and is able to serve our waking, conscious soul-life and our capacity to experience. Once again we see that the camera represents only a lifeless caricature of the eye, which itself is an animate organ, imbued with inner activity. Through this activity, it becomes a living mirror of the soul. Through a person's eyes the very soul looks out at us and reveals its inner self to us, its innocent purity or silent love, its distress or excitement in tears of pain or joy.

But what helps the eye to counteract this necessary catabolic process? One of the great mysteries of the eye is that it is always ready, that it somehow manages to stop up all the holes we have described, repairing the damage, and reproducing visual purple. 'The faded retina becomes red again through the regeneration of the visual purple as soon as it is kept in the dark for a period of time. In the case of total fading (i.e. after a strong impression of light, W.B.) it takes 30 to 40 minutes,' writes Professor Rein in his book on human physiology.

What helps to see again and look into the world refreshed? The lower man with his anabolic processes of metabolism. The nerve sheath regenerates itself by letting the forces of the blood flow through it! In order to rebuild what is destroyed in seeing, the eye must have blood. We begin to see how complex the functioning of such an organ is. Every sense organ is made up of highly specialized, delicately structured nerves, with nerve endings and all that they entail. The eye has rods and cones; for example, at the very centre of the retina, the yellow spot, where vision is clearest, there are 14,000 nerve-cones in every square millimetre! But even this is not enough. Blood must always enter to counteract through anabolism the catabolic process associated with every sensation—whether of sight, hearing, smell, taste or touch.

This anabolic process takes place at the unconscious level, so that we are usually unaware of it, just as we are fortunately unaware of the hole-formation in the retina. This process of anabolism, which, as we know, takes place best in the dark, is like a little nap for the eye, during which it can regain its strength.

In some cases, however, we do become aware of anabolism to a small extent. If, for example, you look at the red setting sun, and then at a white surface, you see an annoying after-image. But you may notice to your surprise that this after-image suddenly turns another colour, namely green. Or take a large piece of white paper and fasten a round disk made of red paper on to it. Under good lighting conditions concentrate on the centre of the disk for two minutes. Then remove the red disk and continue looking at the white paper. You will then see the after-image, the negative 'hole-image', filling up with green, the complementary colour of red. This is just magnificent: an ethereally soft, delicate colour, such as you usually find only in the rainbow, is now produced by the eye.

For every sensation of colour the eye seeks a complementary sensation through its mysterious inner activity. It has the ability to transform every perception of colour, to complement it in a meaningful way. The coolness of green is added to red, which is warm; cool blue is added to radiant yellow-orange, and so forth. So for each colour there is a corresponding complementary colour, which the eye itself forms. Here again we see that the eye is anything but a lifeless camera. The eye acts creatively, imaginatively and artistically, thus sharing unconsciously in the creative impulse of the whole man, who does not merely reflect the world and take it passively. Within itself it is active and productive; it wants to add something to the world, to supply something that was·missing, the *creative* after-image. We must distinguish between the negative after-image that is passively formed, and the positive after-image that is newly created by the eye and meaningfully transformed through its own activity. Fortunately, we are usually unaware of this activity, too, for if we always noticed everything the eye was doing inside us, we should never be able to see clearly.

The eye even creates complementary movements, counter to those it has passively received! There is an interesting experiment that shows this phenomenon, though it hardly seems possible. Watch something that is moving in a specific direction—a centripetally rotating disk, for example. When you remove the rotating disk, which you have looked at for three minutes, you will notice that centrifugal counter-movements suddenly appear. If you then look at a drawing of a tree, it does not remain still, but actually appears to expand! This is one of the strangest experiences you can have. It is a fact that a specific movement in a particular direction is transformed by the eye into the opposite movement. We can remember one thing: the eye not only passively reproduces the image it receives, but it also actively creates an after-image; it tries in a delicate way to create anew, through counter-movements and complementary colours.

But what is it that works so creatively in the eye to form after-images in complementary colours and movements? It is the blood; it is the life-force that is continually flowing into the eye via the blood!

Let us summarize what we now know. The basic parts of the eye are nerve and blood, retina and choroid membrane. When we see, a hole-like, negative after-image is formed in the retina. Through the blood, this hole is filled up again, the eye is regenerated. In the soul-life of the eye, the creation of the delicate, complementary after-image is closely associated with the organic regeneration of tissue in the retina itself.

*

Because the eye, as we have seen, is equipped with its own tiny piece of 'brain', we can learn from it something of the general functioning of the brain. Connecting the eyes with the brain are two large nerves that cross behind the eyes in complex fashion before reaching the hindbrain. Here, at the back of the head in the cerebral cortex, these nerves take on a very delicate, complex structure. Corresponding to each of the sense organs is a special section of the brain, where the sensations we perceive are further processed. All that I have described so far is the process of perception, of sensation. And here we experience something astonishing, which we cannot take for granted: from each sensation that we perceive or experience, from every image we see, a second after-image is formed, which has no direct relationship (though there is an indirect one) to the after-images of the retina.

What do I mean by this? Look at the green square in Figure 5. Now cover it up. Though you can no longer see it with your eyes, you know exactly how it looks. You bear the image of the square within yourself, and would be able to draw it without looking at the diagram. This is only possible because you carry it within you. Hours from now you will still be able to recall this image of the green square, though it is long since out of sight. We form inner images of everything we see, hear, perceive, and experience—delicate after-images. During our life or even in the course of a single day, we build up a magnificent treasury of images. We all know what this treasury is called: the memory.

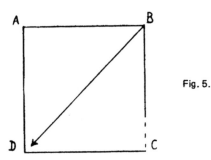

Fig. 5.

Whenever we bring an image out of the treasury of our inner self, whenever we reproduce such an image, we remember. That is, we reach into our self and bring something out, an image we were able to take in only through the eye or some other sense organ. There is something quite extraordinary about this image: the first after-image we considered, of the sun, for example, is produced by the retina, and we cannot change it. Nor can we change the creative green after-image of the red setting sun. It remains there as long as the eye can continue to form it. Once it has disappeared, no power on earth can bring it back again. It is gone. But the other after-image, the memory-image, despite its delicacy, has a much greater permanency.

Here, in the memory, we experience one of the functions of the brain. For only because we have a brain, and because the retina of the eye is connected to it, are we able to create new, inner images. And these images are free floating. We ourselves bring them out whenever we wish, for they are part of our life of soul.

We cannot say that the after-image in the retina is part of our conscious soul-life, because it is a physiological process, a fact of the organic life of the sense organ. The memory-image, on the contrary, is part of the foundation of our life of soul; its form will be accurate and clear the more we make the effort to be inwardly attentive to our original perception as it occurs. The memory is really the foundation of the soul and makes possible everything else in our soul-life—all our purposeful endeavours, aspirations and thoughts. Memory-images originate in the functioning of the brain. The brain is also what reflects them inside us when we remember. For when we picture something within us, we need an inner mirror—the mirror of the brain.

In the brain's creation of memory pictures we find the retina's activity of forming after-images magnificently transformed. Just as nervous tissue is necessary to the formation of the eye's after-images, so too is it necessary in the brain, for the creation and reflection of these memory pictures.

We have seen that the eye's 'private brain', the retina, not only can create a new after-image from one passively received from outside, but it can even transform this image and give it a new colour through the forces of the blood working upon the retina. We must ask at this point whether the brain itself might also be capable of making creative changes in the images it receives. The answer is not difficult, we are all capable of inwardly transforming a green square into a red or yellow one. But we can also inwardly change this square in another way. For example, we can draw an imaginary line from one corner of the square to another, from the second corner (B) to the fourth corner (D) (Figure 5). Or we could say, 'This square is badly drawn; it has a hole in it (at corner C) that I don't like; I'll correct it inwardly.' We then draw—I do not know whether we need a piece of soul-chalk for this purpose—the rest of the square. Thus each of us is capable of transforming the after-image of the memory. The fact that we ourselves can at any time, as we wish, recall and change the inner green square, making it glow in any or all colours—not just in one complementary colour, as in the eye—shows that our brain's soul-forces are no longer bound up with bodily processes. They have become independent. This is a very important observation.

If we study this ability to transform images we become aware of something magnificent in ourselves. For this ability to transform images, to make them grow within us, to colour or reshape them, gives us also the potentiality of creating totally *new* images. We can cause a tree to grow within us; we can make it blossom: we can hang cherries or apples on it—whatever we wish. A person who has no house can build within himself a four-storey home with balconies and bathrooms; we can build and elaborate whole dream castles in the soul. The name we give to this activity sums all this up in an extremely abstract way. For what are names in comparison with the real life within us! Nevertheless, we need such names if we are to make ourselves understood. What, then, do we call this ability to create images within ourselves? We call it *imagination*.

We are now acquainted with two fundamental aspects of our soul's activity in the nervous system, with two capacities that are entirely different, yet closely connected: memory and imagination.

*

We can freely, at any time, summon up an after-image from the memory and set it before our souls, so to speak. In German, this activity of ideation is even called *Vorstellung*, a 'setting before', or re-presentation. We know that the brain must act as a mirror if we are to form such a mental image; yet, we must not confuse the mirror with the image. None of us is so foolish as to think that the table or the bouquet of flowers reflected in a mirror is inside it. Only small children believe this. And we should be equally unwise if we believed that memory-images are contained somewhere inside the brain. For they are made neither of nervous tissue nor of phosphorous, oxygen, or nitrogen. They are purely soul-images, and made, if you like, of 'soul-matter', though this is a rather peculiar concept. But however we choose to express it, one fact remains certain: these images are *not* made of physical brain-matter. They are woven from the same light we described as the 'light of the eye'. The brain itself serves merely to reflect the abundance of our soul-images and memory-images.

At this point we must ask *how* the brain helps us to develop our imagination, enabling us to transcend the basic memory image—changing it, adding to it, and improving it as we wish. What comes from within the organism to meet us? For the soul, despite its relative independence, always needs certain physiological processes as its basis. We must therefore ask: What is behind the activity of the imagination, what comes from within the body to help us, so that, using our imagination, we can create images in the innermost part of our soul?

We are aided here by the same element that helps the eye to create coloured after-images or to resynthesize the visual purple that has been destroyed in seeing. We are aided by the blood circulating through the brain, by the blood's life in the nervous system. The brain alone would be sufficient merely to reflect images; but in order to transform these creatively, the soul needs the life of the blood flowing through the nervous system. The force we need to hold a memory or a mental image before us, to reflect it in our inner mirror, is the formative power of ideation, of memory, which is part of the force of thinking. In order, however, to move an image, to recast it, we need something quite different. The simple force of ideation is not enough.

To make this difficult point understandable, let us observe the movements of our hands. For example, in order to hold a sponge still in front of me, I must hold my hand in a specific way and freeze it, so to speak, in that position. For this I need calmness. Inwardly, too, I can the better hold an image before me, the greater my calm, the greater my power to hold still, and the greater the concentration with which I inwardly reproduce it. The brain is capable of accurately reflecting our ideas only because it has this stillness, only because its convolutions are no longer in motion and its thousands of nerve branches, bifurcations, and ramifications do not sway back and forth like the branches of a tree, but are as motionless as crystal, a blanket of snow, or the smooth surface of a body of still water. We must recall this point once more: in the brain the activity of pulsating, mobile life is brought to a standstill as much as possible. The brain sacrifices much of its life and vitality; its cells do not even reproduce themselves. All such activity has been brought to a halt. We have already described this process, which enables the brain to be a true mirror. It is the same with my hand. If it began to move, the sponge would fall to the floor. Similarly, if the brain moved, all memory images would either become distorted or disappear. We would not be able to set them before us properly.

But my hand has another alternative. It can alter the sponge I am holding. It can squeeze it and release it again; it can move it all around; it can change its shape. What am I doing? I am using my will. In order to move something in the outer world, to guide it in different directions, to change its shape, to alter it, I always need the soul force of the will, a force whose instruments are in this case my arm and its muscles.

But what soul force do we need to alter the delicate memory-image, to move it, or even to 'drop' it—we call this forgetting—and bring out a new one? The soul-force of the will! It may sound strange at first that the will is active in a way that does not use the limbs, as when we drive a nail with a hammer or change the shape of iron on an anvil. In imagination we make use of an internally freed will, one that has been released from its bond with the body. And as will freed from the body, it can be effective in a purely *inward* way: moving images, altering and reshaping them. This will-force of the soul participates in the activity of the imagination just as the force of ideation permits the simple holding of a memory-image before us.

In investigating these two basic soul functions we must be aware that behind the force of ideation is the ability to *reflect* and behind the imagination is the creative will-force that enables us to *transform* images continually and to create new ones in our soul. Deep down, on the physiological, organic level, it is the marvellous, crystalline stillness of the brain, composed of nerve tissue, that enables us to form an idea of something calmly and accurately. And behind the inner activity of will and imagination is the creative life-force of the flowing, pulsating blood, inwardly set in motion. For just as the brain must be rigid to serve as a mirror, so must the imagination be inwardly mobile, sustained by something that is itself in motion: the flowing, streaming blood, which itself is capable of continual self-change.

*

We have now discovered that the whole man is found again in the head. In ideation, we try to picture the world and ourselves as clearly as possible. For this we need the head, with its sense organs and brain. But because we are not content merely to reflect the world passively, but also want to act in it and change it, even our head must have a share in the creative power of willing. Even its external appearance reveals this ability of the head to carry out actions of the will—at least with the lower jaw and tongue, where it has retained last vestiges of limb activity. It is this soul-will that enables us to move and transform images and ideas. So we perceive that even our mental activity is bound up in the antithesis, the great inner tension, the polarity we have found in the body as a whole.

Let us carry our observations a step further. We are able to see through our eyes only because a 'hole' is made in the retina; in the brain, too, when mental images are formed, nerve substance always undergoes catabolism. Whenever we have an idea, whenever we hold an image before us in our souls, a kind of hardening takes place in the brain; a minute hard structure, an organic counterpart seemingly of crystal or salt, is formed. So when you picture the square in your soul, a delicate impression, an organic, physical one, is left in the mirror of the brain. In time, such impressions begin to 'oversalt' the brain, as it were, making it even more rigid and lifeless than it already is. These structures accumulate during the day, since we form an incredible number of mental images, all of which the brain must reflect. So the brain becomes increasingly oversalted and rigid. By evening we begin to notice this process as a feeling of fatigue.

The eye is equally incapable of reversing completely all the catabolic processes that take place in it during the day. Here, too, catabolic residues accumulate, just as they do in the entire sensory-nervous system. We could almost say that these salty incrustations eventually 'fall out' of the living organs, until, by the end of the day, these have become as perforated as a sieve. It is as though the hard knots in solidly constructed wood panelling came loose and fell out, leaving knot-holes behind. So the eye is tired in the evening, the head and brain are dulled, and we can no longer cope with ourselves.

At this point, the nervous system must call upon the blood, which always helps to reverse the results of catabolic processes. It must now wash away all the catabolic residues in the brain and help to rebuild it. But until the brain has agreed to send the soul away, so to extinguish its mirror-images for a time, the blood cannot renew and refresh it. The brain agrees—and at that moment we fall asleep! For when the same anabolic process that refills holes in the retina takes hold of the whole sensory-nervous system, we fall asleep.

Only by viewing it in this way can we understand sleep, which is a phenomenon of the nervous system alone. For who is it that sleeps? Is it the heart? The heart would never consider such a thing; it continues to function. The stomach? It would not think of it, either; it continues to digest. The kidneys, the liver, and all other organs continue to function at night. Only the sensory-nervous system sleeps. Because it is destroyed during the day, it lets itself be healed at night. We could say that the sensory-nervous system is a kind of chronic patient. Every day it becomes ill, and every night we must take it to its private sanatorium—our bed—in order to restore its health with fresh life-forces.

You may already suspect that when the minute, constantly occuring alternation we have observed in the eye, as the breaking-down and building-up of visual purple, takes hold of the whole man, it results in the great alternating rhythm of waking and sleeping. The moment we awaken to our conscious life of soul, physiological catabolism begins in the sensory-nervous system. But while we sleep at night, anabolism takes place through the power of the blood. During this process the blood does not wish to be disturbed by our consciousness.

In the final analysis, the whole man is bound up, through waking and sleeping, in the all encompassing rhythm of anabolism and catabolism that takes place on a small scale in the eye; he is bound up in the great polarity of nerve and blood: in the upper man, the nerve-sense man, who wants to observe, and the lower man, the metabolic man, who wants to nourish, build up, grow, and propagate his species. In sleep, something like creative, refreshing anabolic activity is going on. But it is not merely an after-image in the eye that is created: the image of the whole man is created anew and reborn.

We are sometimes aware of a small fragment of the vast creative activity of the nervous system, just as we sometimes perceive the green after-image of the red setting sun. Sometimes the secret that a wonderful process of anabolism, of formation and transformation takes place during sleep is illuminated for us. When we become conscious of this process, of this image-rich anabolism, we say, 'Last night I had a beautiful dream.' Our dream-life reveals the secret of how sleep renews us with the incredible imaginative force of the blood, with the unconscious strength of creative will. For what is a dream? A magnificent play of imaginative forces that have been freed within us. We know that we can complete a square or draw a diagonal across it, but what is this bit of imaginative play in comparison with the powerful images that dreams present to us in all their colour, variety, and lightning change? And yet, as beautiful as a dream may be, there is often something chaotic about it. We are not quite satisfied with it, we want to leave it and wake up, to be sober and clear-headed, creating and moving small, modest images of our own rather than being overwhelmed by dreams. We want to be fully involved when images arise within us. For if we were not properly involved and the images became too independent, something in us would be disturbed, unsettled; we should not be fully ourselves, and that would be terrible. When are we completely ourselves? When we are *awake!*

But memory, too, is important in dreaming. For dreams would not be possible, if they could not also continually borrow from memory. Much of what we dream we have brought out of the store house of our memory; and when these memories appear, un-bridled and unguided, they are immediately whirled into confusion by the imagination. The reason memory and imagination become independent and go their own ways is that we ourselves are not involved. When we are involved, we place ourselves in the middle, as it were: we take the reins. We are the ones who arrange, organize and summon up the images, and who above all keep memory and imagination in balance. If we did not maintain such balance and relied solely on memory, we should only be able to keep bringing back old images, just as they came to us. Our souls would become mummified. We should not allow anything new to come into being; completely oriented towards the past, we should become tradition-bound pedants. And at the same time we might become too strongly attached to what the material world has reflected into us through our senses. We should become materialists. But on the other hand, when we disregard the accuracy of the memory and become too infatuated with the lack of restraint and the glittering versatility of the imagination, a new danger appears. We again lose our inner balance, and the beautiful activity of imagination becomes fantasy. We begin to fantasize and talk nonsense, the images become blurred and faded, and again we cannot live a clear life of soul. Such one-sidedness in our ideas can actually be the long range cause of serious illness.

When for professional or other reasons a person becomes accustomed to having mainly cold, sober, abstract thoughts—thoughts that are bloodless and colourless—or receiving such thoughts passively from outside, he exaggerates the process of catabolism. His brain is threatened with petrifaction and sclerosis. Over the course of time, his blood becomes less and less able to counteract this hardening, especially if he had as a child dry, unimaginative teachers who burdened his brain with lifeless facts. This hardening process is hastened if as an adult he loses sleep because of overwork. At first, the head defends itself against the impoverishment of its inner life-forces by removing them from its periphery and becoming prematurely grey or even bald. But if this process of premature ageing spreads inward to the brain, the person becomes senile. Suffering from sclerosis of the brain, he loses the ability to remember, for the mirror of his brain has become blinded, as it were, through incrustation.

This and other degenerative processes of the nervous system are speeded up even more if this person, through habit or outside pressure, burdens his nerves with still other superfluous processes of catabolism—if, for example, he leaves the radio on without listening to it consciously or if the advertisements in the subway burden his eyes without interesting him. Any sensations that we do not receive consciously and assimilate with interest make us nervous and tend to destroy our nervous system. They dissipate our soul-forces inwardly. For this reason the organism becomes increasingly unable to combat, through the blood's anabolic processes, the one-sided, incorrect functioning of the nerves. So the person develops insomnia, a condition that is spreading like an epidemic in our civilization.

*

Adequate sleep and a balanced diet are not enough to keep the nervous system healthy. We must also care for our life of soul, especially our conscious activity of ideation, in a corresponding way. We do this best when we develop our memory and imagination equally, continually balancing their two opposing natures and uniting them harmoniously.

For this purpose we need a third force, one that functions in our consciousness as the heart does in the body as a whole. It is this heart force that we shall now consider.

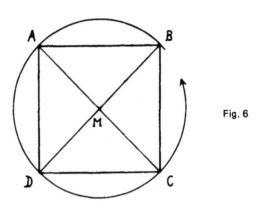

Fig. 6

Let us again observe a figure with four equal sides, a square (see Figure 6). Aided by the versatility of our imagination, which we shall not allow to have free rein but shall limit to the figure, let us join the four corners with two new lines, the diagonals a and b. They intersect at a new, fifth point, M. What kind of point is this? Around it are grouped four right-angled isosceles triangles, all of which are obviously of the same size. Because the two equal sides of each triangle are all the same length, point M is equidistant from all four corners of the square. It occurs to us that M is the centre of the square. From the store of our memory, let us now bring out the idea of a circle; in our imagination, we can exactly circumscribe it around the square, if its radius corresponds to the size of one of the equal sides of the triangle, or half a diagonal. Its centre is identical with that of the square. Accordingly, every square can be inscribed in its corresponding circle.

We can see that the imagination was at work here, as well as the memory—but both were under strict guidance. As a result, something completely new has come into being in our understanding of the relationships among the lines and figures we have drawn. What are we actually doing when we deal with images, joining them together in this way? We are *thinking*, we are accumulating thoughts! If we now ask, what balances imagination and memory, exact reproduction and versatile, free transformation, so that we do not go through life as if in a chaotic dream, the answer can only be, the power of thinking, as everyone can experience himself. In *Faust*, Mephistopheles says of thinking that it is the heavenly light in man; he calls it *reason*. Even Mephistopheles knows that in thinking the innermost core of man's being shines forth as an immortal, divine spark. Yes! *Heavenly light* becomes active in us when we think. It illuminates in us the relationships that exist among things. Things that had seemed obscure become clear to us and are revealed from a new point of view. As we experienced to a limited extent in our drawing of a square, thinking gives all the images of our soul an inner structure and invests them with a new splendour.

In thinking, we become *enlightened* about the nature of the world, and we *comprehend* its regularities. Indeed, thinking endows our ego with an inner, spiritual *eye*. With it we gain an inner insight, just as we see physical views and perspectives with our outer eyes. The breadth of our inner horizon depends on the clarity and activity of our spiritual eye. And as our external vision is dependent on the retina and choroid membrane, so thinking as inner vision is physically dependent on the nerves and blood in the brain (see Figure 7). It thereby unites the power of memory and the activity of the imagination, throwing a high arched bridge across the chasm of their polarity, a bridge that rises even into the realm of the spirit. On this bridge, our higher I-nature meets us as the inner guide who alone is capable of finding the golden mean we have been seeking in our observations of thinking, feeling and willing. Clear, vivid thinking that yields itself up unselfishly and courageously to the spirit extends its healing influence not only into our soul life but even down into our physical body.

In conclusion, let us summarize our observations. When we perceive, our soul is rooted in the material world of the body, in the sensory world of matter. In remembering and imagining, however, the soul lives and grows in its own subjective inner world and is full of activity. If in so doing it trusts in the power of thinking, it then opens self-confidently to the world of the spirit and blossoms within the light of truth. Thus the ways in which we all live in the light of the world are manifold. For through the portals of the senses we open to the light of the outer world, while

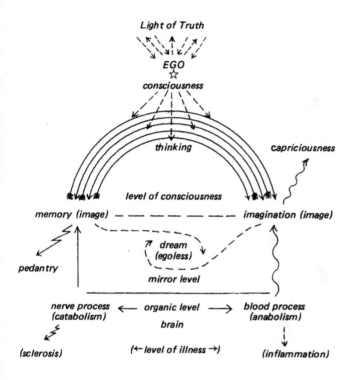

Fig. 7. Diagram of Brain Function

inwardly we open to the light of the spirit; between these two, the light of our soul is active in the colourful play of memory and imagination, saying, with the guardians of the tower in Goethe's *Faust*, that we are all:

> For seeing intended,
> Destined for sight;
> The tower, our home;
> The world, our delight.

But the world upon which we look is itself both inner and outer. Our observations have led us to appreciate this fact, and to see ourselves as citizens of both.